Bordeaux mixture

Charles S. 1852-1929 Crandall

UNIVERSITY OF ILLINOIS
Agricultural . Experiment Station

BULLETIN No. 135

BORDEAUX MIXTURE

By CHARLES S. CRANDALL

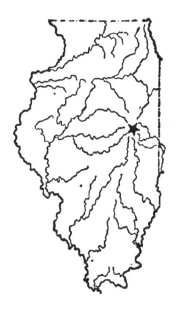

URBANA, ILLINOIS, MAY, 1909

1. Bordeaux mixture was discovered by accident in the fall of 1882 by Professor Millardet.   Page 205

2. Original formulas have been greatly modified. The first formula contained more than six times the copper sulphate and nearly 12 times the lime per gallon of water that is used in the present standard 4-4-50 formula. Page 207

3. It is conclusively demonstrated that mixtures made with air-slaked lime are not only extremely injurious to foliage, but are much less adhesive than are mixtures made with fresh-slaked lime.   Pages 210 and 288

4. The chemical reactions that occur when copper sulphate and lime are combined take place in a manner to give best results only when the ingredients are combined in certain definite proportions. Hence formulas should be strictly followed.   Page 212

5. Equal and full dilution of the milk of lime and the copper sulphate solution, before mixing, gives mixtures that are least injurious and of maximum adhesiveness.   Page 213

6. With all precautions taken injuries to foliage sometimes occur and are not to be avoided. In such cases injury is usually associated with unfortunate weather conditions.   Page 215

7. Rightly made Bordeaux mixture is remarkably adhesive. When once dried on the leaves it is not easily removed by rains, but continues its defensive action for long periods.   Page 217

8. There is decided advantage in the maintenance of an excess of lime on the leaves. This must be accomplished by subsequent applications of milk of lime and not by additions of lime to the original mixture.   Page 218

9. There is no evidence indicating danger to orchard trees from accumulation of copper sulphate in the soil as a result of spraying.   Page 219

10. Well made Bordeaux mixture contains no copper in solution, but small quantities of copper become soluble very soon after application to foliage. The presence of free calcium hydroxide, in large excess, retards, but does not entirely prevent solution of the copper.   Page 225

11. Bordeaux mixture on foliage yields soluble copper more rapidly under the action of meteoric waters than under the action of waters artificially applied. Injury to foliage follows the action of rain in some cases, but does not result from water artificially applied.   Page 226

12. Physical condition of leaves at time of spraying is important. Leaves injured by insects, or attacked by fungi are especially susceptible to additional injury by Bordeaux mixture.   Page 233

13. Epidemics of the trouble known as "Yellowing of leaves" appear to have no relation to weather conditions and no evidence has been found that Bordeaux mixtures causes yellowing. Experiments do show definitely that copper sulphate solutions cause yellowing and that the degree of yellowing depends upon the strength of the solution.   Pages 234-237

14. Healthy bark of trunk and branches is impervious to Bordeaux mixture and to solutions of copper sulphate.   Page 238

15. Copper sulphate solutions varying between 1:100 and 1:1000 when absorbed by trees, thru wounds, invariably kill the leaves which then become brown.   Page 238

16. In one instance absorption of a solution 1:25000 was followed by yellowing of leaves.   Page 240

17. Examinations of drip waters from sprayed trees show the early appearance and continued presence of copper in solution. They also show the extreme adhesiveness of Bordeaux mixture and the slow solubility of the copper.
Pages 260-262

18. Conclusions.   Page 292

BORDEAUX MIXTURE

By CHARLES S. CRANDALL, Associate Professor of Pomology

INTRODUCTION

Methods of warfare against fruit pests—fungi, bacterial diseases and insects—have developed in a wonderful manner during the last few years. The devastations of parasites have forced upon fruit growers the conviction that strong effort in the direction of efficient control is the only salvation for the fruit business.

The idea of making applications to fruit trees to check or prevent the ravages of insects and diseases is by no means new. Remedies for fruit tree troubles were recommended by early writers and it seems probable that their use may be as old as fruit culture. Early remedies were mainly of the nature of repellents, substances which, on account of bad odors, caustic, or other disagreeable properties, were thought capable of driving away insects or warding off disease. In a few cases, perhaps, applications were made before invasion and with the definite purpose of preventing attack, but more frequently applications followed the discovery that serious injury had been inflicted, and were made in an endeavor to check further injury by driving away the invaders. These applications were made, generally, with very imperfect knowledge of the organisms responsible for the injury and without tangible basis for the belief that the nostrums used were in any degree effective against the particular organisms causing the injury. It follows, that, while there were frequent reports of benefit, the major portion of efforts expended in the application of supposed curative substances failed to give relief, or in any way diminish the losses. The treatments here referred to were those of the early days before orcharding had developed as a distinct business. Fruit plantations were, in the main, small, mostly home farm orchards. Applications were intermittent, desultory, without much system and never on an extended scale.

Out of the first crude efforts have grown systems of procedure based on principles that have been worked out thru detailed investigations of particular parasites and thru carefully planned and skillfully executed experiments with remedial applications.

Those investigators who have specialized on the problems relating to the control of fruit parasites are now able to recommend materials and practices from the basis of often repeated tests, and to predict results with reasonable confidence. Always, however, with the express reservation that climatical or atmospheric conditions may greatly modify or entirely reverse the results obtained under normal conditions. Altho advancement has been great, it can not yet be said that the business of combating plant parasites has reached the limits of development. Evolution is still going on. Old problems are modified, new problems appear, and new materials are suggested for trial; so that changes in procedure are constantly occurring and the practice of spraying, considered in its entirety, must still be regarded as in a form-ative stage, rather than as bounded by definite and distinct lines of practice. When it is considered that little more than two decades have passed since the beginning of systematic effort to control the parasites in commercial fruit plantations, it is evident that there has been great progress toward the mastery of these problems. It is also apparent that the experiences of each season increase the general understanding of the problems, and improve the effectiveness of remedial applica-tions.

The present state of efficiency, it should be understood, has not been reached over a perfectly smooth and unobstructed course. There have been difficulties to overcome. Records of experiments with ma-terials and methods do not show an unbroken sequence of successes. There have been failures, results have been negative, mistakes have been made. Trees have been defoliated and fruit has been ruined. These things have served as retarding agencies; but considered with the aggregate of successful operations they become mere incidents such as should be expected to.attend any large undertaking.

The chief difficulty attending the use of applications for control of diseases and insects has been, and still is, that the compounds applied too frequently exert an injurious action upon foliage and fruit. Thru the whole course of development of spraying practices, the absorbing problem for both pathologists and entomologists has been the discovery of substances which, while possessing high efficiency as fun-gicides and insecticides, are at the same time harmless to foliage and fruit. Many substances known to possess high value as remedies . against particular parasites can not be used at all because of equally destructive action upon the host plants. Even the most approved of modern remedies are not uniformly harmless. In careless hands, they very frequently inflict serious injury, and in the most careful hands, their harmlessness can not be absolutely depended upon.

Injury to foliage and fruit by materials applied as spray, has often discouraged beginners and called forth the resolve to pursue the prac-tice no further. But such a course is unwise. Experience has taught that control of parasites is essential to the production of marketable fruit, that spraying is the only means of effecting control, and that in the majority of cases good results attend the practice. The remedy for discouraging results lies in close study of attending circumstances, in more careful attention to the details of preparation and application, in short in discovery of the difficulty and such modification of practice as will prevent its future occurrence.

Investigation of spraying compounds in their relation to foliage in-jury was undertaken by the Department of Horticulture in response to a popular demand for information on the subject. It was commenced in a small way in 1905 and has been in progress since. The work is by no means complete and this bulletin is presented as a report of pro-gress only, and not as a finished treatment of the subject. The prob-lem is complex, presenting many distinct phases. On the physiological side are questions bearing upon the direct effects of various sprays upon plant cells and upon the development of those changes that result in the injuries observed; also questions involving the delicate processes of plant assimilation and nutrition and the relation of spray compounds to these functions. On the chemical side are included determinations of the composition of commercial materials, and of the compounds formed in making the various mixtures used in spraying; the changes occurring in spray mixtures after deposition upon the plants, and the presence of foreign substances in affected tissues. In most cases the quantities dealt with are extremely minute and, in general, the chemical work is of such delicate nature as to call for a high degree of skill and a perfect equipment.

With the experience of each season, new anomalies are presented out of which grow new secondary problems that add to the difficulties of the major problem. One of these problems is the relation of spraying to atmospheric conditions and the varying phenomena attendant thereon. Experiences here are varied and perplexing; so much so that several seasons will be necessary to fully test the complications arising thru atmospheric influences and to correlate them in such manner as would warrant definite conclusions that could serve to guide practice.

HISTORICAL

The list of really important substances or mixtures used as insecticides and fungicides in commercial orchards is not a long one and some brief consideration of the introduction and development of these remedies may not be out of place here. Arsenical poisons have been the chief remedies used against insects and of these Paris green came into use some time previous to 1870 and London purple was introduced in 1871 or 1872. Both these substances were used as remedies for the Colorado potato beetle which at that time, was destroying the potato crop over a large portion of the country. Strong objections were urged against the use of these poisons because of supposed danger to human life, but their efficiency as insecticides and the absence of fatalities following continued use of potatoes as food soon resulted in their general acceptance as successful remedies.

The prejudices held against the use of arsenical poisons on potatoes were even stronger in regard to proposed applications of these substances to fruit plants. Extension of use was thus considerably delayed, but as early as 1872 the use of Paris green for canker worm on apple trees was reported in a few cases. The earliest application of Paris green as a remedy for codling moth appears to have been in 1878 in New York, but altho entire success was reported it was some years before applications for this purpose became general. In 1881, Professor Cook stated before the Michigan Horticultural Society (Report 1881, p. 131) that he had used Paris green successfully on a few trees of his own, but he would not then recommend it to others because of the dangerous nature of the substance. By the year 1886, Paris green had advanced to first rank as an orchard insecticide and its use on a large scale still continues. More or less serious injury to foliage commonly attends the use of Paris green, and has been present since its first introduction. This trouble is less now than formerly, because better grades of Paris green are obtainable, and because of the common practice of combining it either with lime alone or with Bordeaux mixture containing lime in excess. Still, it sometimes causes injury notwithstanding precautions taken to render it safe. London purple has always been destructive to foliage, and, for this reason, is now seldom used against orchard insects.

Arsenate of lead has steadily grown in favor during the last few years and is now quite. extensively used. (This preparation was the outcome of an effort on the part of the Gipsy Moth Commission of Massachusetts to find an arsenical poison to replace Paris green, since Paris green frequently caused serious injury to foliage). It was first used in 1893. Its fine division, its ability to remain long in suspension in water, its adhesiveness, and its insolubilty are all strong points in favor of this compound, and were it not for its somewhat higher cost it would soon entirely supersede its present rival, Paris green.

FUNGICIDES

During the early years of fruit growing in this country, little trouble was experienced from parasitic fungi, but as years passed certain diseases became troublesome. The fruit most seriously affected was the grape. During the years preceding 1850, grape culture assumed large proportions, and considerable areas, in regions supposed to be especially adapted to grapes, were given up to this crop. Between 1850 and 1860, the devastating action of the grape diseases known under the names of rot, blight, and mildew increased year by year and many vineyards that were, at first, profitable, were entirely destroyed. The threatened ruin of the grape industry turned attention to remedies and many things were tried, but no successful means of combating the trouble was discovered.

In 1878 the Downy Mildew—*Peronospora viticola*—a native American fungus originally parasitic on wild grapes, was introduced into France, and in the years following did enormous injury to the vineyards of the more important wine producing districts. The Powdery Mildew—*Uncinula spiralis*—had long been a pest in French vineyards, as in those of this country, and had for years been successfully controlled by the use of sulphur, but the new disease because of its entirely different manner of growth did not yield to the sulphur treatment, and relief was sought in the use of a great variety of substances. Finally a remedy was discovered, the introduction of which marked the beginning of a new era, not only in grape culture, but in the culture of many other fruit crops.

DISCOVERY OF THE FUNGICIDAL ACTION OF COPPER

The discovery that compounds of copper possessed fungicidal properties was made as long ago as 1807. In that year it was proved that copper sulphate in dilute solutions, would prevent germination of spores of wheat smut—(*Tilletia tritici*).

Benedict Prevost, published at Montauban in 1807 a memoir, on the immediate cause of smut or rust in wheat and gave details of a series of experiments, with results obtained. On page 60 is the following—"Thus the actual sulphate necessary to give to the water the power of preventing the rust from germinating, at a low temperature, does not exceed 1/400,000 of its weight, and 1/1200,000 retards its germination."[1]   This discovery does not appear to have been largely used in practice and there is no suggestion of extending its application to control of other fungi. During the following 50 years there is occasional reference to treatment of seed wheat by copper sulphate solutions. In 1861 W. F. Radclyffe, reasoning from his knowledge of the fact that "solution of vitriol was a sure remedy for smutty wheat seed, applied with a watering pot, to rose bushes affected with mildew a solution of 2 ounces of blue vitriol to a stable bucket of cold water. The receipt signally succeeded, and the Geants are perfectly cleaned of the mildew."[2]   Evidently the successful treatment here reported was not repeated as no later mention of it is to be found. No further experiments with copper compounds are reported until we come to those of Millardet.

DISCOVERY OF BORDEAUX MIXTURE

What was first known as the "Copper Mixture of Gironde" and later as Bordeaux mixture—the "Bouillie bordelaise" of the French—was discovered by accident in the fall of 1882 by Professor Millardet of the Faculty of Sciences, Bordeaux, France.

The following is the account of the discovery as given by Professor Millardet:[3]

"Since the appearance of mildew in France, 1878, I have not ceased to study *Peronospora* in the hope of discovering a weak point in its development that would permit mastery of it. The results of my observations are to be found recorded in various publications. I had noticed, in the course of my researches, that the summer spores, or conidia of the *Peronospora* readily lost their power of germinating. This observation and the failure of all the treatments that had been attempted, resulted in the formulation of this conclusion—that a practical treatment of mildew ought to have for its aim, not the killing of the parasite in the leaves which are infected, that which seems impossible without killing the leaves themselves, but of preventing its development by covering the surface of the leaves with various substances capable of causing the spores to lose their vitality, or at least hindering their germination."

"Three years ago I was searching for a substance which would answer the purpose that I had outlined, when chance placed it in my hands. The last of October, 1882, I had occasion to pass thru the vineyard of St. Julian in Medoc. I was not a little surprised to see that all along the route which I followed the vines still bore leaves while every where else the leaves had long since fallen. There had

[1]Comptes Rendus 101 (1885) p. 1225.
[2]Gardener's Chronicle 1861 p. 967.
[3]Jour. d'Agr. Prat. October 8, 1885, pp. 513-514.

been some mildew this year, and my first impulse was to attribute the persistence of the leaves along the road to some treatment which had preserved them from the disease. Examination enabled me, indeed, to ascertain immediately that the leaves were in great part covered, on the upper surface with a slight adherent coating of a bluish-white pulverulent substance." .

"Arriving at the Chateau Beaucaillon I questioned the manager, Mr. Ernst David, who told me that it was the custom in Medoc at the turning of the grape to cover the leaves with verdigris or sulphate of copper mixed with lime in order to keep away marauders; they, seeing the leaves covered with coppery spots, were not bold enough to taste the fruits hidden beneath for fear that they had been contaminated with the same matter. I called the attention of Mr. David to the fact of preservation of leaves, which question was discussed and I made him share the hope, which this observation raised in me, of finding in the salts of copper the basis of the treatment of mildew. Mr. David at first, I ought to say, made several objections, but in the end he nevertheless entered completely into my ideas and assisted me in so efficient a manner that I owe to him the best part of the final success."

The year following (1883) Professor Millardet made numerous experiments testing various compounds against the mildew and all these experiments were duplicated by Mr. David on the estate at Medoc. These experiments were repeated in 1884, but owing to the fact that the mildew did not develop that year, gave no definite results. The results in 1883 were successful in demonstrating the efficiency of the Bordeaux mixture as a remedy for Peronospora and (after publication in the spring of 1885 of the formulas used), the Bordeaux mixture was applied on a large scale by several proprietors of large vineyards. Wherever the mixture was used the mildew was held in complete control. So successful were the results that the remedy at once gained general favor and its use extended rapidly.

We do not know the origin of the use of the copper lime mixture as a protection against trespassers, but the custom had been in vogue for some years. The mixture thus used was of the consistency of thin mush or porridge and was applied to the vines by sprinkling it on with a small broom. The first mixtures made for use against mildew were based upon the original mixture and were too thick to allow application by spraying with a pump and in the fine state of division which later came to be considered desirable.

During the year 1885, and in the following years, notably 1887, the horticultural and viticultural journals, and the reports of societies, published many articles on the general subject of spraying, on the numerous compounds both liquid and dust form, that were tried, and particularly on Bordeaux mixture, which seemed everywhere to stand in greatest favor, because it gave the best results.

There was some controversy over the priority of discovery and several claims were made adverse to Millardet. But Professor Millardet in an article on the history of copper sulphate as a remedy for mildew, appears to have fully established his claim of priority of discovery and of interpretation of the action of the mixture.[1]· No further counter claims appeared and he has since been regarded as the discoverer and introducer of Bordeaux mixture.

FIRST FORMULAS

Of the various formulas used by Professor Millardet in his experiments, the one that gave the most satisfactory results was first published[2] by him in the spring of 1885, and was used that season in many vineyards with entire success. The composition is as follows:

"In 100 litres of whatever water (well, rain, or river)—dissolve 8 kilos of commercial sulphate of copper. In another place make with 30 litres of water and 15 kilos of fat stone lime, a milk of lime which is mixed with the solution of copper sulphate."

Converting this into pounds and gallons we have:

8 kilos copper sulphate	17.6366 pounds
15 kilos lime	33.0687 pounds
130 litres water	34.3421 gallons

This is a little more than one half pound of copper sulphate to the gallon, and almost one pound to the gallon of lime; or more than six times the copper sulphate and nearly twelve times the lime per gallon of water, that is used in making our present standard mixture on the 4–4–50 formula.

At an early stage in his work on the copper compounds, Millardet enlisted the services of his colleague, Mr. U. Gayon, a chemist, and they worked together on numerous problems that developed out of the experiments. In the spring of 1887 they published two articles jointly[3] in which a considerable reduction in the proportion of copper sulphate used, is recommended. During the summer of 1887, field experiments were carried on in three large vineyards in quite widely separated localities. These experiments included a comparative test of mixtures of five different strengths, ranging from the mixture used the previous year consisting of

Copper sulphate	6 kilos
Lime	12 kilos
Water	100 litres

(which stated as we now give our formulas would be approximately a 24.9–49.9–50 formula) down to a mixture made with

Copper sulphate	1 kilo
Lime	340 grammes
Water	100 litres

(or stated in our terms, a 4.1–1.4–50 formula). In this last the lime used is the minimum amount necessary to precipitate all the copper sulphate, and the authors show that while theoretically this is a safe and effective mixture, practically it is not so, because of the great liklihood of using impure lime, thus leaving in solution copper which would be destructive to foliage.

---

[1]Journal d'Agriculture Pratique, December 3, 1885.
[2]Annales de la Societe d'Agriculture de la Gironde, April 1, 1885.
[3]Journal d'Agriculture Pratique, May 19, pp. 693–704; May 26, pp. 728–732, (1887).

In the experiments, the mixtures containing the reduced amounts of copper proved equally effective with the strong mixtures, and recommendations were made accordingly.

Report of the experiments was published in three articles in the Journal d'Agriculture Pratique, issues of May 3, 10, 17, 1888. In concluding this report the authors say—"So then, and this is our conclusion, of all the liquids proposed for the treatment of mildew, the most active, the least expensive and the only one the application of which may be absolutely without danger for the vine, is the Bordeaux mixture composed after our new formulas."   (Page 693.)

From the year 1887, Bordeaux mixture was widely and very successfully used in the wine producing districts of France for control of the grape diseases.   Its use was also extended to potatoes for control of potato blight.   Beyond these two crops, however, the French appear to have found no general application for Bordeaux mixture.

INTRODUCTION OF BORDEAUX MIXTURE IN THE UNITED STATES

Thru the Department of Agriculture Bordeaux mixture was introduced in this country in 1887.   Agents of the Department conducted experiments testing various compounds for control of grape diseases and a number of individuals tried the remedies recommended by the Department.   Circular No. 3 sent out by the Department in May 1887, gave formulas as reported in French Journals:

Copper sulphate...................................... 8 pounds
Lime...10 pounds
Water...20 gallons
                              and
Copper sulphate....................................16 pounds
Lime...30 pounds
Water...28 gallons

Directions for making mixtures on this last formula end with this remark: "Some have reduced the ingredients to 2 pounds of sulphate of copper and 2 pounds of lime to 22 gallons of water and have obtained good results".[1]   On page 43 of Bulletin 5 (1888) this remark is made—"In regard to Bordeaux mixture, it has been found that when the amount of sulphate of copper contained in it is less than 6–8 percent, its efficacy is materially diminished.   The old formula (water 22 gallons, sulphate of copper 13 pounds, lime 26 pounds) is the one still held to be the best.   The 'new formula' or 'mixture for general application' consists of:

Water...22 gallons
Sulphate of copper................................. 6 pounds
Lime.. 2 pounds

Good results have been obtained with this mixture, but it is advisable owing to the often impure character of the lime obtainable, to increase the proportion of this substance."

[1]U. S. Department of Agriculture Bulletin 5, 1888, p. 40.

MODIFICATIONS IN FORMULAS

Galloway in his report for the year 1888 gives the formula:

Copper sulphate..................................... 6 pounds
Lime............:.................................... 4 pounds
Water...22 gallons

During the seasons immediately following, this formula was used more than any other. But as the possibilities of the mixture came to be better understood, and its application was extended to plants other than the grape, the conviction grew that reduction in strength was desirable, and in many cases necessary because of the tender nature of the foliage to be treated. Hence a great variety of formulas has been reported. Of seventeen stations reporting in 1891, nine used the 6–4–22 formula; two used 6–4–25 formula; two—Ohio and New Jersey used 4–4–50; the first mention I find of this formula. The other four each used a different formula, but all were weaker than the first given above. Of seventeen reporting in 1894 only one—Rhode Island, used the 6–4–22 formula, while nine used 6–4–50; three used 4–4–50 and four various still weaker mixtures.

By 1896 the 22 gallon formula had disappeared and the custom of stating formulas, on the basis of water content fixed at 50 gallons, came into use. The amount of copper sulphate has varied and still varies between two and six pounds while the lime remains in the majority of cases at four pounds. The Mississippi Valley and regions west accepted the 4–4–50 formula as a standard some years ago, somewhat earlier than did most eastern fruit sections. Within the past two or three years, however, there has developed a well defined movement towards a still further reduction in strength. Right practice calls for just such strength as will do the work—control scab and blotch on apples; scab, curl and brown rot on peach; brown rot and shot hole on plums, and so on. Material applied beyond this is waste. Success has in some cases attended the use of mixtures very weak in copper; in other cases such mixtures have failed to accomplish the purpose of application. In still other cases standard mixtures have failed to give the satisfactory results usually expected. It is, therefore, not surprising that men of experience sometimes doubt their own judgment and hesitate in making choice of a formula. The formula is one factor, time of application is another, and prevailing weather conditions at time of application are of even greater importance. If it were possible to forecast correctly weather conditions spraying operations could be adjusted to insure a maximum of good results, but weather possibilities can not be predetermined with certainty. Hence the safe thing to do is to provide as far as possible for contingencies and leave the matter of formulas to be adjusted according to circumstances that seem best at the immediate time of application.

The immediate success of Bordeaux mixture as a preventive of the ravages of parasitic fungi attacking the grape led to a wide extension of its uses and its universal adoption as the standard remedy for the long list of fungi injurious to orchard, garden, and field crops. In combination with either Paris green or arsenate of lead it is used in practically all of the orchards and small fruit plantations in the state. It is therefore an important factor in the business of fruit growing and every phase of its relations to the plants treated is worthy of consideration.

Serious injury to foliage and fruit sometimes follows the application of sprays as has already been mentioned. Why do these injuries occur? Why do no injuries occur in very many cases? What are the conditions attending the infliction of injury? What are the inciting causes? Are the injuries preventable? These are some of the questions that are woven into an investigation of Bordeaux mixture in its relation to fruit plants. The questions are simple, yet they lead among complex chemical reactions and obscure functional disturbances that require infinite patience in observation and care in interpretation.

MATERIALS FOR BORDEAUX MIXTURE

Good materials are necessary to make a safe and efficient Bordeaux mixture.

COPPER SULPHATE.—The copper sulphate should be pure. This ingredient usually contains a small percentage of iron sulphate, but rarely is it present in excess, or in sufficient quantity to interfere with the efficiency of the copper compound. In the spraying work at this Station no difficulty has been experienced in securing copper sulphate of satisfactory purity.

LIME.—There is often difficulty in obtaining lime that slakes well and effects the perfect precipitation of the copper. All commercial limes contain more or less of impurities. If the percentage of calcium oxide is high, the lime is technically known as "fat lime"; this on the addition of water, slakes quickly and completely and will perform its office in the compounding of Bordeaux mixture in an entirely satisfactory manner. If, however, the lime contains a large percentage of magnesia, or clay, or sand, it is known as "poor." Such lime slakes slowly and incompletely and does not make a satisfactory Bordeaux. Limes from the same quarry are variable and for this reason a given brand will at one time be perfectly satisfactory and at another time unsatisfactory. This uncertainty regarding the purity of lime makes necessary the use of a greater excess than would be necessary if pure calcium oxide could be obtained, or if there was perfect uniformity in the composition of commercial lime.

Under no circumstances should lime that is at all air-slaked be used. Several comparative tests between mixtures made with air-slaked lime and those made with fresh water slaked lime have given positive and uniform results, demonstrating conclusively that mixtures made with air-slaked lime are not only extremely injurious to foliage, but are much less adhesive than are mixtures made with the fresh-slaked lime.

Several brands of "hydrated" or "new process" lime have been placed on the market. Three of these have been tested in the making of Bordeaux mixtures for application to orchard trees. These limes are in an exceedingly fine state of division, much like flour, and are readily suspended in water. The precipitate, in Bordeaux mixture made with "hydrated" lime, remains in suspension equally as well as in mixtures made with fresh-slaked lime. In this respect there is no difference in the limes. However, the process limes are not so satisfactory as are fresh-slaked limes for two reasons: first, the Bordeaux made with them is somewhat less adhesive, and second, in a comparative test, side by side, the Bordeaux made with process lime caused more injury to leaves than did the ordinary Bordeaux made with fresh-slaked lime. Doubling the quantity of hydrated lime does not materially reduce the injury to foliage, but still further reduces the adhesiveness.

As the experiences of each season are correlated and studied the conviction grows that the character of the lime is an important factor in the compounding of a proper Bordeaux mixture. The use of fat stone lime as fresh from the kiln as it is possible to get it, is commended, and it is suggested that where possible, tests be made of the slaking qualities of available brands and the results allowed to govern the decision as to which will best serve the purpose.

WATER.—The question has been raised whether for making Bordeaux mixture, pond water, carrying in suspension a considerable amount of silt, is as desirable as cistern or well water. Several comparative tests have been made. To spray large commercial orchards large quantities of water are necessary and it is essential that the supply be ample and conveniently located. To supply the demand, excavations are made, in the orchard, or as near as surface contours will allow, and so situated that surface waters can be conducted into them and there stored for use at the time for spraying. These pond waters are always considerably discolored by the abundant sediment held in suspension. In comparative tests of mixtures made with pond water, clear cistern water, deep well water and distilled water, nothing to the disadvantage of the pond water was discovered. The pond water Bordeaux has a dull greenish color due to the sediment. In settling tests in the laboratory, pond water Bordeaux stands between that made with distilled water, which settles most rapidly, and those made with the two other·waters which settle at practically the same rate, but the differences are so small that they may be disregarded. Pond water Bordeaux is as adhesive as are the others, equal in efficiency, and considering the advantage of convenience, is to be preferred to any other source of supply.

MAKING BORDEAUX MIXTURE

No less important than the character of the ingredients is the manner of making Bordeaux mixture. The formulas commonly recommended have grown out of experiences and carefully made comparative tests of almost all possible combinations. They can be depended upon as being the best now known and are within reach of everyone. Formulas are entitled to some respect because they represent the thought and labor of experts. The man of experience in spraying may find it desirable to modify formulas to suit special conditions; this he may do with safety, because he is careful to maintain proper proportions and exercise the usual care in preparation. For the beginner it is much the safer plan to follow the formulas as given.

Not infrequently the man of little experience is inclined to place higher value upon his own judgment than upon carefully determined formulas and resorts to estimates for determining quantities of ingredients to be used, or, attempts to follow formulas fail through carelessness in manipulation. In either case, grave mistakes are likely to occur. Very many cases of serious injury to orchard foliage have been traced directly to carelessness or inattention to the details of determining quantities of ingredients, or to the manner of combination of these ingredients. It is also a mistake to do the work in what chances to be the most convenient method, without reference to correctness of the method.

It should be remembered that in the combination of lime and copper sulphate chemical reactions occur and that these reactions take place, in a manner to give best results, only when the ingredients are combined in certain definite proportions; hence adherence to these proportions, which are expressed in the formulas, cannot be too strongly urged.

For the proper making of Bordeaux mixture certain essentials in the way of barrels or tanks and necessary tools should be provided beforehand. The kind of equipment will depend upon the extent of the spraying operations in prospect. For the small home orchard, requiring only small quantities of the mixture a few oil barrels as containers and a small slaking box will serve every purpose; for the larger commercial orchard, where spraying is done from one or more two hundred gallon tanks, every device that will diminish the labor and save waste of time should be employed. Here the elevated platform, so located with reference to pond or well that water can be pumped direct to the diluting tubs is an essential feature. This platform should have two parts, one higher than the other; on the lower part is supported a receiving or mixing tank of somewhat greater capacity than the spray tank, at such distance above the ground as will allow delivery of the mixture, by gravity, to the top of the spray tank driven underneath. The upper platform should be large enough to accommodate two diluting tubs, four or more barrels for stock solutions, and a slaking box, and still leave room for convenient operation of the pump. It should be elevated above the lower platform to such height that the diluting tubs can be adjusted to deliver the solutions together thru a strainer into the receiving tank.

The equipment provided, we may now give attention to the details of mixing. Stock solutions of copper sulphate and lime should be prepared in advance. Fill an oil barrel with 50 gallons of water; then suspend in the water a coarse sack containing 50 pounds of copper sulphate. This gives a solution of definite strength—1 pound to the gallon. The quantity of copper sulphate can be doubled if desired, giving a solution of 2 pounds to the gallon; however, the "pound to the gallon" solution is the one most frequently used. Solutions thus made will keep indefinitely, if protected so that the water does not evaporate. The amount prepared should be adjusted to the extent of the operations. In like manner, prepare a milk of lime which shall contain a definite weight of lime to each gallon of water. Where 50 or more pounds of lime are to be slaked at one time, the shallow box is to be preferred to the barrel, because it affords better opportunity to control the slaking. The success of the mixture depends in great part upon the manner in which the lime is slaked. The two common faults observed in practice are:-the addition of too little water, which results in the development of too much heat and the "burning" of the lime. In this case there are many small lumps that do not completely slake and will be thrown out when the lime is strained into the tank. The second fault is the addition of too large an amount of water resulting in "drowning" of the lime. This, likewise, results in incomplete slaking, and therefore, a reduction in the actual amount of lime added to the mixture. In some cases where the lime is neither perfectly fresh nor of great purity these losses may so reduce the amount that the copper is not all precipitated and serious injury follows. Lime, during the process of slaking should have constant attention; water should be added in small amounts as needed to keep the action even and to insure that perfect slaking which can be obtained in no other way. It is best to slake a definite number of pounds and when thoroly slaked transfer to a barrel containing such amount of water as, added to the quantity used in slaking will give a milk containing a definite quantity of lime to the gallon. Having the stock solutions prepared, the next step is dilution preparatory to mixing.

The diluting tubs should each have capacity, in excess of one hundred gallons. A palm oil cask of 250 gallons capacity, cut in half, will supply two tubs that serve the purpose admirably. We will suppose that the standard 4–4–50 formula is to be used and that the mixture is to be made in lots of 200 gallons. In one diluting tub, place 16 gallons of the stock solution of copper sulphate, made up 1 pound to the gallon, then add 84 gallons of water. The first lot should be carefully measured and the height at which it stands in the tub marked, so that in filling for succeeding mixtures, it is only necessary to fill to the mark. Thoroly agitate the milk of lime and, if it has been made up 1 pound to the gallon, transfer 16 gallons to the other tub and fill up with water in like amount as for the copper sulphate solution. We now have 100 gallons of copper sulphate solution and an equal quantity of milk of lime. This is on the plan of full dilution before mixing, which has been shown by experience to possess advantages over other ways of mixing, such as adding a concentrated solution of copper to fully diluted lime, or concentrated lime to fully diluted copper sulphate, or combining the two ingredients in concentrated form and then diluting. By this method of equal and full dilution before mixing, the chemical action between the copper sulphate and lime appears to take place quicker and more completely, than by the other methods. The resulting mixture settles less rapidly, is less frequently injurious, and attains a maximum of adhesiveness. These points of difference have been determined by field and laboratory experiments with mixtures made in the different ways, and we have no hesitation in urging equal and full dilution before mixing as being the best plan to follow. In mixing, equal streams may be conducted directly into a strainer supported over the receiving tank, or the streams may meet in a short trough which terminates on the strainer. Before starting the streams, the milk of lime must be thoroly stirred and this agitation should continue until the mixing is completed in order to insure uniformity in the combination.

There are a number of small details in connection with a mixing outfit such as has been described, that may be modified in various ways, and cheapened or made more expensive, according to the wishes of the individual, but, while cheapness is desirable the better appliances are likely to be the cheaper in the end. Any device that will economize time, by expediting the filling of tanks, or that will reduce the liability to accidents which result in loss of material is worthy of consideration, and a few dollars expended in this direction are well invested.

It is an unpleasant fact that much spraying is done badly; this means that much money is thrown away. Such waste is believed to be avoidable because it has its origin in carelessness and inattention to details.

The common sources of trouble in spraying as determined by observation and investigation of many specific cases may be summarized under three heads:

1. Use of impure or improper materials, as, for example an adulterated brand of Paris green which contains an undesirable amount of free soluble arsenic, or of air-slaked lime in making Bordeaux mixture. There is no excuse for the use of air-slaked lime, and trouble with Paris green can be avoided by purchasing a brand of approved merit.

2. Carelessness in making the compounds. Guessing at weights and measures and mixing in the easiest rather than in what has been demonstrated to be the right way. These are easily avoidable sources of trouble for which there is no excuse.

3. Improper and ineffective application. Much material is wasted and possible benefits are lost thru poor work in application. Right application depends upon the man who handles the pole, and, if this man is inattentive, lazy, and in too great haste to finish, an, at best, unpleasant task, there is certain to be uneven distribution; parts of trees within easy reach sprayed in excess and more remote parts untouched. It is difficult to eliminate this source of trouble, because it depends upon the character of the help obtainable, and often this is inefficient and unreliable. The nearest approach to a remedy is reached in as close and constant supervision as it is possible to give.

Of these three sources of error, the first two can be entirely eliminated and the third greatly mitigated, by that reasonable care that is commonly given to other branches of the orchard business. For the attainment of best results, it is necessary to keep clearly in mind the purpose for which the spraying is done, and to respect the smallest details that promote good work and count for efficiency.

But even when all known precautions have been taken and everything possible done to promote success, difficulties are sometimes encountered. Leaves are burned, fruit is russeted, and epidemics of chlorotic foliage occur that affect the performance of the trees. These troubles are very frequently complained of, and, while in many cases these injuries result directly from errors in practice, there have been a sufficient number of cases of injury following spraying by experienced and careful men to show that injuries are not always preventable.

THE CHEMISTRY OF BORDEAUX MIXTURE

The chemistry of Bordeaux mixture, the reactions that take place when copper sulphate solution and milk of lime are mixed together, and the exact nature of the compounds formed appears, even at this date, to be involved in some obscurity.

Considerable work on the chemical side has been done, but, so far as I have been able to ascertain, no complete investigation has been reported, such as would clear up all the perplexing phenomena that have been observed in connection with the mixture. Millardet and Gayon,[1] without going into the chemical details, state that the copper, as deposited on the leaves, is in the form of copper hydrate ($Cu(OH)_2$). According to these authors, the copper hydrate deposited remains insoluble until all the calcium hydrate has been neutralized by the carbon dioxide of the air. The time required for this depends upon the excess of lime used in compounding the mixture. Five mixtures were made with varying amounts of lime, the precipitate dried, pulverized, and definite quantities spread on filter paper. These papers were so arranged that when rain or spray was passed thru them it could be caught and examined for copper. The mixture containing least lime yielded soluble copper in four days and as the lime increased the time elapsing before the appearance of copper lengthened to twelve days. These experiments indicate that, in well made Bordeaux, no copper is left in solution.

Chester[2] gives the reactions in making Bordeaux mixture as follows: "In the addition of the milk of lime to a solution of copper sulphate, the lime in solution precipitates the copper as cupric hydroxide forming at the same time a slightly soluble sulphate of lime. These two salts, together with an excess of lime remain in suspension in Bordeaux mixture. The reaction is simple.

$$CuSO_4, 5H_2O + CaO, H_2O = Cu(OH)_2 + CaSO_4 + 5H_2O".$$

In the same year, Professor Livio Sostegni, in an article on the chemical composition of Bordeaux mixture,[3] reaches the following conclusions:

1. "In the so called Bordeaux mixtures prepared with ordinary quick lime there almost always remain in solution small quantities of

[1]Millardet and Gayon. Jour. d'Agr. Prat. May 17, 1887, p. 701.
[2]F. D. Chester. Jour. Mycol. 6 (1890) p. 21.
[3]L. Sostegni, L. Stazioni Sperimentali Agarie Italiane Vol. 19, p. 139. August, 1890.

copper, which in some cases remain undetected by any common reaction, but which are easily recognized and determined by the electrolytic method. The quantity of lime used has an influence; in fact when a large excess is used only very small traces of copper can be detected."

2. "The quantity of copper which may remain in solution is considerably greater when slaked lime is used, or lime which has been slightly carbonated. Also when the lime is added directly to the solution of copper sulphate. If incompletely slaked lime is used, or even lime not well diluted, the quantity of copper which may remain in solution is sometimes considerable, altho the liquid may be decidedly alkaline. The maximum of copper salt in solution is found when caustic lime in the form of powder is added directly to the sulphate solution a little at a time."

3. "The copper is precipitated in the Bordeaux mixture in the form of the hydrate, basic sulphate, and the double basic sulphate of copper and calcium. It seems that in this last form, which is, however, richest in sulphate of lime, the small quantities of copper which are found are held in solution."

The conclusions reached by Dr. Sostegni would be more acceptable had they been reached by using milk of lime, as used in making Bordeaux mixture, instead of lime water. This use of lime water raises the question—would milk of lime give the same result? Fairchild[1] comments on this point and adds "the fact that no mention is made of the changes in color of the mixture corresponding with similar changes taking place when one of the alkalis proper is added to the copper sulphate, also leads to the belief that he has overestimated the proportion of the basic salt present in the mixture as ordinarily prepared."

The direct statement, that the copper, deposited on the leaves in spraying, is in the form of copper hydrate, has been so frequently repeated that it has quite generally come to be accepted as a piece of common knowledge. Occasionally, mention is made of the possible presence of basic sulphates, but most writers, even tho recognizing in their own minds the obscurity of the reactions, prefer the simple accepted statement rather than attempt proof by argument or investigation.

The latest contribution to the chemistry of Bordeaux mixture that has come to my notice is that by Professor Umfreville Pickering[2], Director of the Woburn Experiment Station, England, which appeared in December 1907, and from which I wish to make a brief quotation. "It is remarkable that the nature of the substance constituting this mixture has not yet been elucidated. The reaction occurring is generally represented as resulting in the formation of copper hydroxide altho occasionally it is suggested that a basic sulphate may be formed and an equation is given representing a basic sulphate ($2CuO$, SO_3) which, so far as is known has no existence. That copper hydroxide is the product of the reaction scarcely admits of serious con-

[1]Fairchild, D. G., U. S. Dept. Agr. Div. Veg. Path. Bul. 6 (1894), p. 14.
[2]Pickering, Prof. U., Jour. Chem. Soc. London, Vols. XCI and XCII, 1907, pp. 1988 and 2001.

sideration, for this hydroxide as is well known, loses its water and its blue color in a very short time, turning black, whereas Bordeaux mixture remains quite blue for an indefinite period." "In Bordeaux mixture made with milk of lime, there must be free lime, and generally, calcium carbonate, mechanically mixed with the precipitate, and any direct investigation of the composition of this precipitate would be of little value. Lime water, therefore, was used instead of milk of lime; but even then any analysis of the precipitate was practically impossible, for it is very bulky and difficult to wash whilst water as will be shown, partly decomposes it, as does carbon dioxide."

In summarizing Professor Pickering says—"The substances formed on the addition of lime to copper sulphate as in the preparation of Bordeaux mixture are dependent upon the proportions of lime used and may be either:

1. $4CuO, SO_3, 0.06\ CaSO_4$
2. $5CuO, SO_3, 0.25\ CaSO_4$
3. $10CuO, SO_3, 1.30\ CaSO_4$
4. $10CuO, SO_3, 4CaO, SO_3$

and probably 5. $10CuO, SO_3, 10CaO, SO_3$

or   6. $CuO, 3CaO$

that present in most cases probably 4."

Here again are analyses made with lime water instead of milk of lime, and if, as Professor Pickering says, analyses of the precipitate even where lime water is used is "practically impossible" it seems likely that the exact changes that occur in making Bordeaux mixture are doomed to remain in some degree mysterious, at least for the layman.

ADHESIVENESS

Rightly made Bordeaux mixture is remarkably adhesive. When once deposited on foliage, it does not readily yield to the washing action of rains, but remains and continues its defensive action for long periods. The addition of soap to Bordeaux mixture increases its adhesiveness. This was first shown by Galloway[1] in 1893 in experiments devised to test the effect of the addition of various substances upon the spreading of the mixture on leaves of cereals. It was further demonstrated by Guillon and Gouirand[2] in experiments conducted for the express purpose of testing the relative adhesiveness of mixtures variously modified. They used two sets of mixtures, one freshly made, the other 24 hours after preparation. Both sets were tested on glass plates and also on grape leaves. The authors conclude that adhesiveness decreases with age, particularly in the case of Bordeaux mixtures made with soda, or to which soap has been added. They also conclude that "the compounds are on the whole more adhesive, the nearer they are to being neutral." In the same year (1898), Joseph Perraud[3] reported a test of adhesiveness for 21 combinations of various substances, including Bordeaux mixtures made in different ways.

[1]B. T. Galloway. Experiments in the Treatment of Rusts Affecting Wheat and Other Cereals, Jour. Mycol. VII (1893), p. 202.
[2]Compt. Rend. 127 (1898), pp. 254, 256, 423–424.
[3]Perraud, Joseph. Jour. d'Agr. Prat. 1898, pp. 814–816.

He concludes that the adhesiveness of copper mixtures is much less upon the fruit than upon the leaves of the grape; also that adhesiveness is relatively weak for old mixtures. The mixtures ranking highest in adhesiveness in his experiments appear in the following order.

1. Bordeaux with carbonate of soda—slightly alkaline.
2. Bordeaux with fat lime—slightly alkaline.
3. Bordeaux with equal parts of copper sulphate and fat lime.

A more recent and elaborate test of adhesiveness is that made by W. Kelhofer[1] and reported in 1907. It was found that under the influence of artificial rain, or of short natural showers, the Bordeaux mixture made with carbonate of soda possessed greater adhesiveness than did Bordeaux made with lime; but, under a long continued gentle rain Bordeaux, made with lime, took first rank in adhesiveness. The author ascribed the difference to the action of certain constituents of the atmosphere and of rain water, particularly ammonium nitrate and carbon dioxide. These constituents, acting singly, or together, exert a stronger solvent action upon the soda Bordeaux than upon the lime Bordeaux. By experiments, it was determined that, as between the two constituents named, the carbon dioxide exerted much the greater action, and also that alkaline Bordeaux was much more adhesive than neutral or nearly neutral mixtures. Kelhofer's final conclusion is "that Bordeaux mixture with a moderate excess of lime, say about 1 kg to 2 kg of copper sulphate can be recommended under all conditions."

It is now quite generally accepted that the benefits that accrue from the addition of soap and other substances are not sufficient to warrant their use in compounding mixtures for use in commercial orchards. Bordeaux mixture without additions when well made, is, at once, the most adhesive and the most efficient of all substances that have been used on any extended scale as preventives against the attacks of parasitic fungi.

Adhesiveness depends very much upon the making of the mixture, and attention to this cannot be too strongly urged. Variation in the proportions of copper sulphate and lime, beyond certain well defined limits, decreases adhesiveness. Insufficient lime, or lime of poor quality, or lime that is in any degree air-slaked will not give a maximum of adhesiveness. Neither will too great an excess of the best quality of lime. The proportions giving greatest adhesiveness are fairly well indicated in the formulas accepted for general use. Those mixtures are best in adhesiveness, and in efficiency, in which an approximation of equal parts of copper sulphate and lime are maintained. This has been demonstrated over and over again in the experiments conducted by this station. That there is decided advantage in the maintenance of an excess of lime upon the foliage is also clearly shown by our experiments, but this excess must be provided by subsequent applications and not by increasing the proportion in the original mixture. When Bordeaux has once dried down upon the leaves, further additions of lime do not affect its adhesive qualities, but, if lime is

---

[1]Kelhofer, W. Zeitschrift fur Pflanzenkrankheiten 17 (1907), pp. 1–12.

used in greatly increased quantity in making the mixture, it has a decided influence in diminishng adhesiveness.

ACCUMULATION OF COPPER IN THE SOIL

Bordeaux mixture applied to trees in spraying eventually finds its way into the soil and the fear has been expressed that the accumulation of copper in the soil will in time result in injury to the trees. This possibility was suggested some years ago by owners of vineyards in France and several investigators instituted experiments bearing upon the question.

Millardet and Gayon cite[1] the fact that M. Garros, proprietor of a large vineyard deposited annually for ten years, large quantities of copper sulphate about the bases of his grape vines in an attempt to control Phylloxera. The amount was between 5 and 10 grams per vine per year which would represent from 44.6 pounds to 89.2 pounds per acre per year. The vines showed no effects, but continued to grow and fruit in a normal way.

Girard[2] reported to the French Academy in 1895 the results of a series of experiments extending over three years. He estimated the amount of copper deposited in the vineyard in one season at 13.38 pounds per acre; he assumes that in 100 years the quantity would be 100 times as great or 1338 pounds per acre. This amount he added, at one time, to a plat on which was grown wheat, oats, clover and beets. The planting extended over an adjoining plat of equal area, prepared in the same way, but not treated with copper. Comparison of the crops harvested from the two plats serves as a basis for his conclusion, which is expressed as follows: "The agricultural results that I have just made known being added to those that other experimenters have already published, demonstrate in a certain manner that the repetition during a very long time, during a century, of the treatment of the grape or potato, by copper mixtures, has no influence either from the point of view of the abundance of the harvests, or in respect to their quality."

That large amounts of copper sulphate in the soil act injuriously upon plants has been shown by Beach[3] who grew peas, tomatoes and wheat in prepared soils containing 2 percent and 5 percent by weight of copper sulphate. Germination was less rapid in the prepared soils, than in the check soils, altho the number of seeds germinated was greater in the prepared soils. Plants on the prepared soils were of a darker green color than were the control plants, but they were much dwarfed, matured earlier and yielded less. The roots of the plants on the prepared soil made very little growth as compared with the plants on normal soils. In these experiments the amount of copper sulphate added to the soil is excessive; far beyond any possible accumulation that could result from spraying as practiced in commercial orchards.

The possible amount of copper sulphate that may reach the soil in the commercial spraying of one season is from 1/1200 to 1/1500 the

[1]Jour. d'Agr. Prat. May 19, 1887, p. 704.
[2]Girard, Aime. Compt. Rend. 120 (1895), p. 1147–1152.
[3]S. A. Beach. N. Y. Sta. Bul. 41. 1892.

amount in the soil containing 2 percent as used in the experiments referred to above. Orchards that have been sprayed for a number of years have shown no deterioration that can be ascribed to the presence of copper in the soil. It has been suggested that accumulations of copper in the soil are responsible for the epidemics of yellow leaves, but there are, as yet, no definite observations or experiments that serve to support this suggestion.

INJURIES TO FOLIAGE

The injuries which have been under consideration at this station are: First—the burning or "brown spotting" of parts of leaves. Second —the yellowing and falling of leaves.

Just what relation these two injuries have to each other cannot be definitely stated. In certain cases, yellowing appeared to supplement browning. Badly brown spotted leaves became yellow and fell. In one case, of 1000 yellow leaves gathered under a tree, that had been sprayed with a solution of copper sulphate, each leaf had several to many brown spots, or else had some portion of the margin browned.

On the other hand, leaves, free from brown spots, may become yellow and fall. Yellowing is commonly epidemic in character and may occur on the same trees three or four times, during a season. Brown spotted leaves may turn yellow and fall, or may persist, and the uninjured portions may continue to perform their functions until the end of the season. The beginning of yellowing appears to prompt the completion of the absciss, or separative layer, at the base of the petiole, and, within 48 hours, the leaves are ready to drop at the slightest touch. A shower of rain, during an advanced epidemic of yellowing, will greatly change the appearance of affected trees, by the removal of all yellow leaves. Yellowing is more serious than brown spotting because affected leaves are entirely destroyed. It is also more erratic in appearance and duration, and presents more anomalies in development. The causes, too, are more obscure and more difficult to prove.

BURNING OR "BROWN SPOTTING" OF LEAVES

The leaf injuries most frequently observed and most often the cause of complaint from orchard owners, are brown spots, within whose limits the tissue is dead. These spots appear on a portion of the leaves, or, in bad cases, on practically all leaves. They are usually sharply delimited, and may be irregular or often circular in form. Sometimes the part affected may be the tip of the leaf, or it may be a narrow line along the margin. The dead areas or spots may be few or numerous, large or small. They may or may not increase in size, after first appearance. If little or no increase in size occurs, surrounding parts may remain green and the leaves continue to perform their functions, altho their capacity is diminished, in proportion to the amount of tissue affected. In some cases the brown spots on many leaves increase until the leaves die. In other cases, while not entirely killed, leaves are so badly affected, and perform so small a part of their normal functions, that growth is checked and preparation of buds for the following year is nearly suspended.

Trees need their full complement of foliage in order to make proper growth, ripen the wood, and prepare for the crop to follow; hence the loss of any portion of the working leaf surface is detrimental and such loss should be prevented if possible. While spray mixtures often cause such brown spotting as is described above, it must not be assumed that all brown spotting is the result of spraying. Other causes produce similar injuries and it is a common mistake to ascribe to spraying, injuries for which spraying is in no way responsible. Late spring frosts and high winds, accompanying cold storms, are sometimes accountable for the browning of foliage, as was the case in many orchards in the spring of 1907, and again in 1908. The injury noted was of uneven distribution, being most pronounced where exposure was greatest and gradually decreasing until it disappeared in the more protected portions of the orchards. Leaf tips and margins were most affected but often there were irregular browned areas, disconnected from the marginal injury. Certain fungi, as for example *Spheropsis malorum,* often mark the leaves of apple trees with brown spots, that in the early stages may be mistaken for the injury from spraying. The color of the spots is the same, but there is a certain regularity in form that does not belong to injuries inflicted by spraying, and this regularity forms a ready means of distinction. Moreover, as the spots become older they assume an ash gray color that easily distinguishes them from spots resulting from spray. A considerable number of orchards, in Marion, Clay, and Richland counties, exhibit this form of brown spotting from fungi. Leaf eating insects often eat holes in leaves or consume marginal strips, and, as the exposed edges turn brown, the injuries are mistaken for spray injuries.

The occurrence of brown spots on foliage that has been sprayed varies greatly with individual trees. Vigorous, healthy trees are often free from injury, while the weaker, less vigorous, are as often seriously injured. There is, too, a difference in susceptibility to injury and this difference varies with the seasons. In some years, owing usually to unfavorable weather, foliage comes out in a condition of general debility and is easily injured by agencies that, in other seasons, would be harmless. Again, there may be an early and abundant infliction of apple scab and after it there is great certainty of serious brown spotting from spraying.

One other cause contributory to brown spotting by spray is deserving of mention and that is what may be termed the minor insect injuries. These injuries are inflicted by a great variety of insects, and they are of such a nature as to escape casual observation; yet, in the aggregate, they are serious, because they render the leaves liable to greater injuries by spraying. Numerous field trials have shown that brown spots result after the direct application of spray compounds to broken places in the leaf cuticle. The same compounds, namely, Bordeaux mixtures, solutions of copper sulphate, white arsenic, and Paris green suspended in water, are found to exert the poisonous influence very slowly, and very often not at all, on leaves having un-broken cuticle. These experiments, taken in connection with the fre-quent injury observed, lead to the opinion that fruit tree leaves are often not nearly so free from these minor injuries as is likely to be inferred from casual examination.

These injuries are naturally most abundant in uncultivated or-chards and in those where lack of care allows undisturbed harbor and breeding ground for all kinds of insects. · As illustrating the preva-lence of these small injuries, it may be stated that critical examination of 6000 leaves, taken at random from 60 different trees, gave only 27, or less than ½ percent of absolutely perfect leaves, altho the gen-eral appearance of the foliage on these trees was good. This last phase of leaf injury needs further study than has yet been given it, but the facts thus far gathered emphasize the necessity of controlling early attacks of apple scab and indicate that minor leaf injuries should re-ceive more attention.

SPRAYING AS A CAUSE OF BROWNING OR BURNING

Having mentioned the various causes other than spraying that directly or indirectly produce the brown spotting or burning of foliage, we may now return to spraying as a cause. Injuries, directly caused by spraying, do occur, and have occurred, ever since copper compounds and arsenites were first applied to plants. Millardet frequently re-ferred to injuries to foliage, and all writers, who treat of spraying, have more or less to say on the subject. The ideal spray compound that will be perfectly effective against orchard pests, and, at the same time, perfectly harmless to foliage, on all occasions and under all con-ditions, has not yet been discovered. Of all the various preparations used, Bordeaux mixture most nearly approximates the ideal, but its harmlessness cannot be absolutely depended upon. Many experiments have been conducted in the endeavor to find means for insuring harm-less action, but up to the present time results have not been univer-sally successful. Differences of opinion have arisen among experi-menters regarding the exact manner in which injuries occur, and even regarding the particular ingredients of the mixture that cause the injury. Some have held that injury should be ascribed to the caustic action of the lime, particularly in cases where applications have been made to young foliage. Most investigators, however, now agree that brown spotting, resulting from Bordeaux mixture, is caused solely by the copper contained therein; but opinions are still widely different as to the exact manner in which the injuries are inflicted. It is essen-tial that the causes of the injuries be understood before preventive measures can be intelligently investigated.

The question is an exceedingly delicate one, and, altho answers have been attempted by several trained investigators, there is still reas-able doubt as to the exact manner in which injuries are caused. There appear to be two important phenomena involved, which, while linked together, the one preceding and essential to the other, are yet separate and distinct. These phenomena are, the solution of the copper and the transmission of the toxic influence to the cell protoplasm. The two problems are then—

First: Under what conditions, and, thru what agencies, does the copper, deposited on leaves in Bordeaux mixture, become soluble? and—

Second: How does this soluble copper establish connection with the protoplasm of the leaf cells, and exert its poisonous influence thereon?

SOLUTION OF THE COPPER IN BORDEAUX MIXTURE

It has already been stated, that, at the time of application, Bordeaux mixture contains no soluble copper. As spread upon the leaves, the copper is insoluble, or at least very slowly soluble. If the copper were absolutely insoluble, its fungicidal power would be inoperative. The mere presence of the metal, while it may be able to inhibit germination of spores in immediate contact with solid particles, would not give the observed protective effect over large leaf surfaces. There must be moisture, carrying a certain percentage of copper in solution, to accomplish the defensive action desired. The agencies, thru which the copper deposited on the leaves becomes soluble, and the rapidity with which solution takes place, are matters that have received attention at the hands of several investigators. The carbon dioxide of the atmosphere is frequently referred to in the literature of Bordeaux mixture as a chief factor in rendering copper soluble. Often the statements appear to imply that it is the only agency in operation. There is very good testimony, supported by direct observation and experiment, to prove that carbon dioxide does have solvent action on copper hydroxide, but it is believed there are other agencies, that, operating alone, or in conjunction with carbon dioxide, are equally effective. The amount of carbon dioxide contained in meteoric waters is extremely minute, and, in cases where relatively large amounts of copper are found in solution, in waters, collected from sprayed trees, it is thought that the solvent action of carbon dioxide may have been supplemented by the action of other agencies. Possibly these agencies are the ammonium compounds, nitrates and nitrites, or some other constituent of the waters or the atmosphere; or the influence may rest in some agency entirely independent of the possibilities here suggested. Results, obtained from some of the experiments made, have suggested some interesting studies concerning the points involved. These studies, it is hoped, can be made during the present year. Millardet and Gayon draw conclusions regarding the effectiveness of carbon dioxide as a solvent for copper hydroxide and in these conclusions make several references to its action. In summing up the results of one series of experiments they conclude that[1] "in the first place it happens that water from rain and dew in consequence of its carbonic acid and carbonate of ammonia dissolves a sufficient amount of copper hydroxide which is on the surface of the leaves, either to completely prevent the germination of conidia of peronospora in this water, or at least it cannot take place in a normal manner."

[1] Jour. d'Agr. Prat. February 23, 1887, p. 161.

These authors held it proved by their experiments that excess of lime in Bordeaux mixture entirely prevents solution of the copper as long as calcium oxide remains on the leaves. "We have proved that the copper hydroxide contained in a drop of mixture is only soluble in rain and dew when the lime which, in the actual mixture is found in enormous excess, is completely neutralized, especially by the carbon dioxide of the atmosphere. As long as a drop of mixture moistened with water shows a perfect alkaline reaction, that is to say, so much so that pure lime is found in solution, the copper hydroxide remains in it in an insoluble state in the meteoric waters.[1]"

This statement by Millardet and Gayon is based upon an experiment which was repeated several times with uniform results. This experiment was as follows:[2] "April 10 we prepared the following five types of mixture.

	No. 1	No. 2	No. 3	No. 4	No. 5
Copper sulphate, grams	16.00	15.00	15.00	15.00	15.00
Lime, grams	3.36	3.36	6.72	13.44	26.88
Distilled water, litre	1	1	1	1	1

As may be seen number 1 contains 1 gram of copper sulphate in excess. Number 2 contains exactly the quantity of lime necessary to precipitate the copper sulphate; analysis showed that there was neither an excess of copper nor of lime. Number 3 contains twice as much lime as number 2. Number 4 contains twice as much as number 3. Finally Number 5 whose composition corresponds to that of the ordinary mixture contains twice as much as number 4. These five mixtures were, at once dried in an oven at 36 degrees C.; then the products of the dessication were finely pulverized in a mortar. Ten grams of each of these dried mixtures was spread in a thin layer of about two millimeters thickness between Berzelius papers supported below by a silk gauze, and tied, at the same time as this latter, on five glass dialyzing dishes of equal opening. The necessary precautions had been taken to determine if the paper and the gauze of the apparatus were capable of absorbing noteworthy quantities of copper."

"April 12th in the evening, these five dishes were exposed in the garden in an open place. From the 13th, they were watered simultaneously by all the rains which fell. When rain did not fall each dish received equal quantities of rain water collected beforehand. The vessels were placed separately on glass funnels which drained into test tubes into which water poured on the dializers was collected. Every two or three days the waters collected from each of the five dishes was removed at the same time, and analyzed separately. The successive order of appearance of the copper in the waters which had passed thru the mixtures was as follows:

Mixture No. 1, April 17
Mixture No. 2, April 19
Mixture No. 3, April 24
Mixture No. 4, April 25
Mixture No. 5, April 30

[1] Jour. d'Agr. Prat. May 19, 1887, p. 700.
[2] Millardet and Gayon. Jour. d'Agr. Prat. May 19, 1887, pp. 701–702.

Other experiments of the same nature made by watering with rain water leaves of spindle tree and of boxwood, previously sprayed with these same five types of mixture, gave similar results. In general, the less lime contained in the mixture the more quickly did copper appear in the water passed over the leaves."

According to these experiments, there is no soluble copper present until complete neutralization of the lime is accomplished. The time of first appearance of copper in solution, in the waters collected, depends upon the amount of lime in the mixture, and varies from 5 to 18 days. It must follow that fungicidal action of the copper is delayed correspondingly, because, only copper in solution is effective in preventing germination of spores. Laboratory experiments at this station, which are given in detail on other pages, gave results that accord with those obtained by Millardet and Gayon in the experiments given above. In these experiments Bordeaux in crystallizing dishes, both dry and intermittently wet, gave no soluble copper at the end of 65 days, and sprayed trees, also dry and frequently moistened, gave no soluble copper to water with which the leaves were washed at the end of 54 days. The experiments of Millardet and Gayon would have been more satisfactory had more explicit information been given regarding the waters that passed thru the mixtures. We are told that "From the 13th they were watered simultaneously by all the rains that fell. When rain did not fall, each dish received equal quantities of rain water collected beforehand." Experiments at this station indicate a remarkable difference in action between direct meteoric waters, and water artificially applied; and it is to be regretted that advice is not given regarding the amount and character of the natural rains, and also of the waters applied artificially in the experiments quoted.

Statements to the effect that fungicidal action of Bordeaux mixture is delayed, are based upon the supposed insolubility of copper hydroxide in the presence of free calcium hydroxide. It is believed, however, that Bordeaux mixture is effective from the moment of application. In repeated experiments, in which spores of *Fusicladium*, in water, were spread on leaves of apple trees, infection was entirely prevented on leaves to which Bordeaux was applied some hours later; while infection was abundant on untreated leaves.

All our field experiments bearing upon the solution of copper hydroxide have given results opposed to those obtained by Millardet and Gayon and to the results of our own laboratory experiments. They show quite conclusively, that while there is no soluble copper present at the time of application, it is, in some way, brought into solution in small quantities, very soon after application; and, further, that copper hydroxide continues to become soluble, even while calcium oxide is still present in excess. As a specific example our tree number 1907 A may be cited. Here the third drenching application of Bordeaux was completed at 11:30 a. m. June 21. Rain amounting to 0.1 inch fell 28 hours later. The water collected carried 14.9 milligrams of copper in solution per litre. Copper was found in measurable quantities in all subsequent waters, but the waters did not become neutral until late in the season.

Comparison of sprayed trees exposed to rain and dew with trees similarly sprayed, protected from rain and dew, and sprayed with cistern water show, by the larger amounts of copper in solution, that meteoric waters possess solvent powers that do not belong to the water artificially applied. It is also clearly indicated by injuries inflicted under meteoric waters, and absence of injury under artificially applied waters, that the mere presence of moisture is not the only essential to injury, but that meteoric waters carry some influence that belongs to them alone, or to them in connection with some other atmospheric condition. The tests with carbonated waters indicate an influence of carbon dioxide, favorable to the solution of copper, but do not point to it as responsible for any increase in injury to foliage.

From those experiments in which sprayed trees were continuously supplied with a large excess of lime, it appeared that injury to foliage was, in part, prevented, altho copper, in solution, continued to appear in the strongly alkaline water collected.

The suggestion is made by several authors that the leaves of sprayed plants may exude some organic substance having solvent action upon copper hydroxide, but the writer has been unable to find proof that this occurs with apple leaves; and efforts to ascertain the truth thru experiments have been thus far attended with negative results only. Swingle[1] suggests that "It is possible that the drops of rain or dew standing for some time on the leaves or other parts of plants may absorb from superficial cells sugar or other substances that may serve to increase the solubility of the copper." Clark[2] makes this definite assertion—"the host plant, too, is active in dissolving the $Cu(OH)_2$". He made an experiment in which matter from leaves of a peach tree sprayed with Bordeaux and having the leaves moistened several times on the previous day, gave a copper reaction; and further, leafy twigs from the sprayed tree soaked some hours in distilled water gave up copper to the water as was determined by a test which gave a marked reaction.

This author further says "the epidermis of leaves, altho protected by a cuticle, is well known to be more or less permeable to the dissolved substances occurring in the cell sap, particularly along the union of the epidermal cells. When the dew is on the leaf we have two solutions—the dew drop without and the cell sap within—separated by a more or less permeable membrane. The result of these conditions must result in the exosmosis of at least some of the contents of the cell sap, which, coming in contact with the copper hydroxide adhering to the leaf surface causes more or less of it to pass into solution."

Bain[3] refers to the varnish like covering of young peach leaves, to the secretion of glands terminating marginal dentations, which, when dried, closely resembles gum arabic, and also to secretions from petiolar glands, but as the result of experiments, concludes "that neither of

[1]Swingle. Bul. 9. Div. Veg. Phys. and Path., U. S. Dept. Agr., 1896, p. 20.
[2]Bot. Gaz. 33 (1902), p. 42.
[3]S. M. Bain, Tenn. Sta. Bul. Vol. 15, No. 2. April, 1902, pp. 53–54.

these secretions can play any important part in producing the injury of copper hydrate to the leaves." From the fact that injury, following application of pure ,basic copper, was confined almost exclusively to marginal teeth, he raises the question "whether this greater marginal injury is due to the greater permeability of the cuticle over the glands or to the mere presence of the secretion there." From other facts brought out in his investigation this author regards it as more probable "that this increased marginal injury is due simply to the greater permeability of the cuticle over the glandular surface of the teeth."

Schander[1] holds the view that the copper on the leaves does not come into solution in any appreciable quantity except under direct action of germinating spores. He says "Upon the basis of my experience I do not believe that enough soluble copper compounds form upon the leaf to kill the spores of fungi, but I assume with Clark that on the whole, fungi dissolve enough copper from the precipitate of Bordeaux mixture adhering to the leaf to kill them." This author also thinks that, in some cases, injury arises from copper that has been brought into solution thru certain atmospheric conditions. He distinguishes three groups of poisonous effects of Bordeaux mixture; first, the plant secretes an acid; this has solvent action on copper hydroxide, which, as brought into solution is taken up by the leaves and injury follows. This is thought to be the case in Fuschia and Œnothera. Second, the secretion is alkaline, but acts as a solvent for copper in the case of the bean (*Phaseolus multiflorus*). The secretion in this case takes place from the glandular bases of the leaf hairs and it is from these glandular bases that injury starts. Bean leaves are especially susceptible to injury by copper salts. Schander expresses the conviction "that the poisonous effect of Bordeaux mixture is always brought about thru the activity of the secretory organs." He expresses the opinion that the injuries observed on peach and sunflower are of the same nature as those observed upon beans. Altho as he says, the possibility of peach leaves secreting a liquid has not yet been proved. Third, "Small quantities of copper salts are dissolved by rain and dew and penetrate the epidermis into the interior of the leaf. Because of the slight solubility of copper in Bordeaux mixture this rarely takes place."

The statements and suggestions regarding the causes operating to bring into solution the copper of Bordeaux mixture deposited on the leaves, as given by the authors quoted above are interesting and helpful, but are not supported, at least, so far as apple tree foliage is concerned, by proof that can be accepted as the final conclusion of the matter. It seems · possible that atmospheric conditions, meteoric waters, carbon dioxide, and leaf secretions may all be concerned in solution of the copper. The results of many recorded experiments and, of our own experiments here, all show great dependence upon atmospheric conditions. This term, atmospheric conditions, is a very convenient cloak for meagre information regarding specific causes affecting solubility of copper, but it is altogether too indefinite and is separable into too many factors to indicate accurate and definite knowledge of the really active agent or agencies.

[1]Schander, R. Landwirtschaftliche Jahrbucher 33, 1904, p. 526.

The term "meteoric waters" is likewise a composite embracing not only the waters, but the materials carried in solution and the relations to one or more of a dozen different atmospheric conditions. Rain water collected in a cistern and artificially applied, gives very different results from those following natural rain and there are wide differences in the observed action of different natural rains upon Bordeaux mixture.

In less degree but no less certainly, there is something of the composite in carbon dioxide as a cause of solution of the copper of Bordeaux mixture, at least there is need of more definite information regarding its action in relation to other factors with which it is associated.

It is not known whether apple leaves give off secretions having solvent action on copper hydroxide. Experiments thus far undertaken have not warranted any definite conclusion and the matter is to be given further study. In attempting to account for the presence of copper in solution, in waters that have dripped from sprayed leaves, and in which free lime is present in quantity, it has been found that these waters contain organic matter. According to Ostwald[1] adding lime in excess to cupric salts in the presence of certain organic compounds e.g. sugar, tartaric acid, glycerine, etc., forms certain complex copper compounds which are not precipitated from solution by alkalies. In certain laboratory experiments, organic matter, in the form of apple leaves macerated in water, added in small quantity to a solution of copper sulphate, used in making Bordeaux mixture, prevented complete precipitation of the copper. The organic matters present in the drip varied in quantity in different waters. The specific compounds have not been determined nor has the origin been ascertained. But, from some of the attending circumstances it is thought possible that secretions from leaves may have contributed. Further experiments are to be made.

PENETRATION OF COPPER INTO LEAF TISSUES

There are differences of opinion regarding the manner in which copper brought into solution on leaf surfaces transmits the toxic influence that kills the protoplasm of the cells within limited areas. The view most commonly held is that water, holding copper in solution, penetrates the cells by osmosis or by a process, of imbibition and thus by direct contact kills them. According to this theory the copper is locked in the dead cells and does not spread through the leaf as would some other poisons. This view of penetration is upheld by Millardet and Gayon[2], Patrigeon[3], Aderhold[4], Schander[5], and others. Opposed to this view, is the theoretical conception, first advanced by Rumm[6] and supported by Frank and Kruger[7], and by Zucker that poisonous action

[1]Ostwald. The Principles of Inorganic Chemistry. Trans. by Findlay, 1902, pp. 532–643.
[2]Millardet and Gayon, Jour. d'Agr. Prat. Jan. 27, 1887, p. 126; Feb. 23, p. 159.
[3]Dr. G. Patrigeon, Jour. d'Agr. Prat. May 5, 1887, p. 641.
[4]R. Aderhold, Jahrsber Angew. Bot. 1, 1903, pp. 26–30.
[5]R. Schander, Landwirtschaftliche. Jahrbucher, 33, 1904, p. 540.
[6]C. Rumm, Ber. Deut. Bot. Ges. Band XI (1893), pp. 79–93.
[7]Frank and Kruger, Ber. Deut. Bot. Ges. Band. XII (1894), pp. 8–11.

results from contact without penetration. Rumm calls the action chemotactic, and ascribed it to electrical attraction between cell protoplasm, and the coating of Bordeaux deposited on the leaves. This theory of action by electrical attraction is based on Nageli's work on Spirogyra, the chlorophyll bands of which were broken up by the near proximity of metallic copper, thru the action of some force to which the name oligodynamic was applied. "Zucker[1] found plants treated with Bordeaux more resistant to etiolation than untreated plants, and partially etiolated plants placed under treatment developed the normal green color. He regards the action as an electrical stimulus and "since in all plants more or less weak electrical currents are produced by the motion of the water in the capillary spaces, it is reasonable that the deposition of a strongly electro-positive substance, like copper hydroxide, upon the leaves should be capable of intensifying the plant currents with stimulating effect upon the activity of the protoplasm." Aderhold and Schander hold the stimulating effect of copper to be only slight and of rare occurrence. Where it does occur, they attribute it to penetration of the cells by the copper, with direct action upon the cells, and the more common injurious effect is attributed to the accumulation of copper, in quantity sufficient to kill the cells.

The supporters of Nageli's theory of oligodynamic action appear to have accepted it, because of their inability to demonstrate the presence of copper within the plant cells. Those who oppose the theory have had no better success in demonstrating the presence of copper in the cells, but hold to the theory of penetration by the copper as more probable than the chemotactic action as proposed by Rumm. Schander[2] credits Rumm with the statement that the amount of copper necessary to produce destructive action on the cells is so small that it is not possible to detect it and adds "An assertion that is difficult to refute and equally difficult to prove." Millardet and Gayon[3] were the first to investigate the behavior of copper on leaves, and their conclusions are drawn from the results of numerous experiments. In one series of experiments, grape leaves were sprayed with 200 grams of a solution of copper sulphate, 2.5 grams to 100 grams of water, and, after being subjected, during one week to rains giving a precipitation of 26 millimeters, were gathered and divided into two lots. One lot was washed ten times with water, the other an equal number of times with dilute hydrochloric acid. Each lot of water was analyzed, and the amount of contained copper determined. Then the lots of leaves were incinerated and the copper in the ash ascertained. Leaves washed with water gave 58.3 percent of the total copper in the ash, those washed with acid 6.1 percent. They conclude from this experiment that "the copper sulphate deposited on the leaves, in the form of very dilute solution, and, in very slight quantity, is absorbed for the most part, and very rapidly, so that the abundant rains are unable to remove it from the leaves." In a later series of experiments these authors digested grape leaves in sul-

---

[1] Quoted from Schander, p. 539.
[2] L. C., p. 540.
[3] Jour. d'Agr. Prat. Jan. 27, 1887, pp. 125–126.

phuric acid for 24 hours, destroying all tissue except the cuticle. The remains were collected, washed free from acid, by prolonged maceration in water, and when neutral, were placed in 100 c.c. of copper sulphate solution, containing 10 milligrams of copper. After 24 hours, the liquid was filtered, and the cuticle placed in distilled water. Finally the particles of cuticle were again collected, dried, incinerated, and copper determinations made, by the electrolytic method, both for the ash, the original copper sulphate solution, and the distilled water in which the particles were last soaked. The copper recovered was as follows:

In solution where the cuticle was soaked 24 hours......0.1 mg.
In distilled water where cuticle was soaked............0.0 mg.
In ashes of the cuticle...............................9.8 mg.
                                                      ————
Total copper recovered........................9.9 mg.

Following this, an experiment was made, to test the rate of absorption. From the two experiments the authors conclude as follows:[1] "These two last experiments show with what rapidity the copper is absorbed by the cuticle, since after only half an hour, half of the copper of the liquid had been absorbed and after one and one half hours in one of the experiments the absorption of this metal was completed." Certain other experiments, designed to test the extension of the influence of the absorbed copper beyond the cuticle, and in which inoculations with spores of *Peronospora* were made on the lower surfaces of sprayed leaves, gave results from which the authors conclude that the copper absorbed by the cuticle extends its influence deep enough into the leaf, to protect in great part from infestation. Finally, from all the experiments this conclusion is drawn—[2] "It seems certain that the copper once absorbed by the leaf is acquired by it in definite manner and can no longer depart from it. Not only is it fixed by the cuticle of the upper face, making that absolutely invulnerable to the parasite, but it is diffused deeply enough in the tissues to constitute a means of protection to the lower surface of the leaf, if not sufficient, it can at least prevent development of the parasite in an appreciable degree."

Absorption of copper, by the cuticle of grape leaves, appears to be demonstrated by these experiments, but the conditions surrounding the experiments are so far removed from normal that it may be questioned whether like absorption occurs under the ordinary practice of spraying and whether Bordeaux mixture would act in the same manner as did the copper sulphate solution, which can not be used in practice, because of its injurious action upon foliage. The solution used in the experiments—2½ grams per 1000 or 1:400—was beyond the limit of safe use on grape vines, according to these authors, who formulate as a law the proposition that[3] "All liquid containing more than one half thousandth (1:2000) of copper in solution is dangerous for the grape vine." The statement that copper, absorbed by the cuticle, is acquired permanently, can not depart from the leaf, and renders it invulnerable is also open to question. If the statement were true the protection

---

[1]Millardet and Gayon. Jour. d'Agr. Prat. Feb. 23, 1887, p. 159.
[2]Millardet and Gayon. Jour. d'Agr. Prat. Feb. 23, 1887, p. 162.
[3]Millardet and Gayon. Jour. d'Agr. Prat. May 26, 1887, p. 729.

would extend thru the season, preventing infection by fungi that develop in late summer. It is well known that apple trees, heavily sprayed in spring and early summer, gradually lose the copper from the leaves and, in seasons of normal rainfall, are readily susceptible to attacks of species of Phyllosticta and often, when conditions are favorable, to renewed development of Fusicladium. These attacks can be prevented by renewed applications of Bordeaux mixture, but, in the absence of late applications, the leaves are attacked. From this it appears, that there can be no copper held in the cuticle or, at least, not enough to prevent infection by fungi which naturally begin or renew development in late summer.

Rumm[1] dwells upon the darker color and the more robust character of sprayed leaves, and, from examinations under the microscope, decides that the deeper color is due to increase in the number of chlorophyll grains. From 47 measurements of the thickness of grape leaves, he finds a gain, in favor of the sprayed leaves, over unsprayed leaves, ranging from 2.17 to 16.31 micromillimeters (p. 84). Regarding causes of the stimulating effects observed, Rumm suggests two possibilities—"Either remains of the sprayed salts are taken up thru the epidermis by the leaf, resulting in chemical changes which appear sooner or later in the above considered physiological changes or the materials only adhere firmly to the cuticle, remain on the whole unchanged and act only by their presence, that is, exert an influence on the life activities of the plant, unexplained up to this time, similar to the influence exerted by light, gravity, etc." (l. c. p. 85).

In order to test these alternatives, grape leaves, sprayed with Bordeaux mixture were washed with dilute muriatic acid, until the wash waters, when tested by the spectroscope, gave no copper lines. Then the leaves were incinerated, the ash dissolved and tested for copper by the spectroscope. No evidence of the presence of copper appeared and from this result it was concluded, "that in our experiments it was highly probable that copper had not been taken up by the leaves in quantity that could be indicated by the spectroscope." (l. c. p. 88). The final conclusion reached by Rumm is expressed as follows: "It is highly probable that the increase in the formation of chlorophyll depends upon a chemotactic attraction which takes place without absorption of the material." (l. c. p. 92).

In an interesting series of experiments recorded by Schander[2] leaves of a variety of plants were used. Each leaf was injured on half its surface by needle pricks, then the leaves were sprayed with copper sulphate solutions in various dilutions. Apple, pear and grape leaves showed no injury from a 1:100,000 solution where the epidermis had not been injured, but were considerably injured where the surfaces had been pricked. The author concludes "that the epidermis of these leaves is capable of preventing the penetration of copper compounds, but that the copper, having once penetrated, behaves towards the protoplasm of the leaf cells, in the same manner as towards the cells of algae and

[1]Rumm, C. Ber. Deut. Bot. Ges. Band XI, 1893, pp. 83–85.
[2]Schander, R. Landwirtschaftliche Jahrbucher 33 (1904), p. 544.

fungi, and can injure the protoplasm in very dilute solutions." (l. c. p. 546).

The only proof of penetration that can be accepted as absolute, is demonstration of the presence of copper within the tissues of leaves that have been sprayed with Bordeaux mixture. This demonstration appears not to have been made, and until it is made, it is only possible to state probabilities as estimated from observed facts. Statements to the effect that penetration occurs, followed by accumulation in cuticularized cell walls, do not appear to rest on sufficient foundation of fact and are not in harmony with the well established fact that extremely small amounts of copper are poisonous to cell protoplasm. If such accumulation occurs, it can hardly apply to other than very minute quantities, unless it be thru chemical changes, which form new compounds, inocuous to the protoplasm of living cells. Again, the presence of accumulations of copper in the cuticle should prevent infection by fungi as long as the leaf lives. But, as has already been stated, leaves sprayed early in the season become susceptible to infection in late summer, unless the protective spray is renewed.

On the upper surface of each of several healthy apple leaves, on one year old grafted trees growing in ten inch pots, were placed in single drops solutions of copper sulphate ranging from 1:100 to 1:1000. The leaves were so adjusted that they could be brought within the focus of the lens for convenient examination. The drops soon evaporated, leaving small masses of crystals. These were again brought into solution by adding drops of rain water. This was repeated twice, or, sometimes, three or four times each day, for two weeks and frequent examinations were made. In no case, did injury to the leaves result, and it was concluded that, under laboratory conditions, the uninjured epidermis of apple leaves was not permeable by copper sulphate solutions.

At the same time, other leaves, arranged in the same way, were treated with the same solutions applied in drops over more or less minute pricks or abrasions of the epidermis. These applications were uniformly followed by injury appearing first as reddish or purplish discolorations, which soon became brown. It is assumed, that breaking the impermeable epidermis established connection between the drop and the exuding cell sap and that thru this channel the copper solution penetrated and killed the cells.

The brown spots were not of equal size, nor were they in all cases co-extensive with the abrasions, or, with the areas covered with the drops applied. Compared with brown spots, resulting from spraying, on the leaves of orchard trees, no distinguishing characteristics appeared. They were identical in appearance and exhibited the same variations in size and form. If the assumption of penetration of copper is warranted, in the case of spots originating in abrasions, there is equal reason for assuming penetration, in the case of the spots on leaves of orchard trees; altho the conditions, making penetration possible, cannot be stated.

Finally, altho actual presence of copper in the dead cells has not been proved, numerous observations have led to a conviction, strengthened by the results of experiments, that brown spotting following applications of Bordeaux mixture is due to the death of leaf cells, and that this destruction of leaf cells is caused by the poisonous action of copper in solution which penetrates to them. The cause or causes of conditions making such penetration possible, are still open to investigation. Out of the great mass of anomalous, often contradictory, results, that have accumulated, it is yet possible to frame a course that will lead to solution of those matters that, at the present time, are obscure and not well understood. The two things that, in the writer's view, stand out most prominently as promising phases of the investigation are—

First. A line of experimentation designed to isolate, as far as is possible, and subject to separate tests, each of several factors included under the term atmospheric conditions.

Second. The physical condition of leaves at the time of spraying.

The importance of this second phase has been suggested by observations made in the field. From inquiry into the circumstances surrounding wide differences in the amount of injury inflicted in different orchards, it appears that, in some cases, differences in materials and methods do not account for differences in injury. It also appears that, in some cases, it is possible to correlate the degree of injury and condition of foliage. Orchards receiving the best care have least injury. Orchards of low vitality induced by general lack of care and by the ravages of insects and diseases, which general conditions tend to harbor and encourage, suffer most injury. It has frequently been observed that late spraying causes more injury than early spraying; and that old leaves are more susceptible to injury than young leaves. It may appear anomalous that young leaves with thin, slightly cuticularized epidermis, should be more resistant than older leaves with fully developed cuticle. But it is believed that such is the case; not because of the thinner epidermis, but because of greater freedom from abrasions that allow penetration of the copper as it becomes soluble. Old leaves have been, for a longer time, subject to the attacks of the numerous insects that infest orchards that are not given good care and are thus made susceptible to injury.

FUNGICIDAL ACTION OF BORDEAUX MIXTURE

The value of Bordeaux mixture as a fungicide rests in the prophylactic action of the contained copper. It has little, if any, curative power. It does not check the growth of fungi, vegetating within plant tissues, but simply prevents germination of spores or arrests growth of germ tubes, and in this manner, checks spread of infection.

It is important that this point be understood and that application of remedies be governed accordingly. If attack of a fungus is threatened, it is necessary that the mixture be applied to the susceptible plants in advance of the appearance of the fungus. Early application with the one aim of defense, is infinitely to be preferred to later applications, intended to check ravages already begun.

Simple solutions of copper sulphate are more effective as fungicides than is Bordeaux mixture, but their poisonous action on foliage puts a ban on their use. Millardet and Gayon[1] made many experiments with solutions of various strengths and they cite the experiences of other investigators. The results all show that even very dilute solutions are not safe to use on foliage. From numerous experiments, at this Station, with solutions of copper sulphate, it is concluded that such solutions have no adhesive qualities, and that the limits of safety to foliage require dilution that renders the solutions inefficient as fungicides.

In the early stages of their work with Bordeaux mixture, Millardet and Gayon studied the action of various copper solutions upon the conidia and zoospores of the grape mildew (*Peronospora viticola*), in order to determine the degree of concentration necessary to prevent infection. This was found[2] to be, for a lime solution 1:10 000, for a sulphate of iron solution 1:100 000 and for a copper sulphate solution 2 to 3:10 000 000. Other investigators have made similar tests, principally with spores of the various rusts and smuts of cereals, and all show that extremely dilute solutions are effective in preventing germination and growth. Spores of different fungi, however, show different degrees of resistance, all do not behave alike in a solution of given strength. For example spores of Penicillium will germinate, and mycelium develop with great vigor in solutions that effectively prevent germination of spores of *Peronospora viticola;* the downy mildew of the grape.

In several tests made here, with spores of the apple scab fungus (*Fusicladium dentriticum*) a considerable degree of resistance has been found. Solutions perfectly effective against grape mildew do not have even a retarding action on growth of spores of the scab fungus. In solutions 1:10 000 germination was effectively prevented. Solutions 1:25 000; 1:50 000 and 1:75 000 did not entirely prevent germination, but did retard growth of the germ tubes in proportion to the degree of concentration.

In a solution 1:100 000, germination was more abundant than in any of the stronger solutions, but, in comparison with the check mount, some retardation of growth was observed here. In still weaker solutions, germination was as free and growth as strong as in the control mounts. In the stronger solution 1:10 000 penicillium grew with apparently undiminished vigor.

YELLOWING OF LEAVES

The causes which produce yellowing of the leaves of apple trees are obscure and not well understood. From observations extending over five seasons, it is thought to be certain that there are several causes which may operate singly, or two or three together in certain cases. The trouble may appear at any time between full expansion of leaves and frost, but has been, usually, more in evidence during

---

[1]Millardet and Gayon, Jour. d'Agr. Prat. May 26, 1887, p. 729.
[2]Millardet and Gayon, Jour. d'Agr. Prat. Nov. 12, 1885, p. 709.

June and July, than earlier or later. Very commonly, attacks of yellowing have been intermittent, occurring two or more times in the course of a season. During the last two seasons, this trouble was not as severe as for 1904, 1905 and 1906. From 1903 to 1906, there appeared to be a gradual augmentation of yellowing and in view of the marked diminution in 1907, and the still less amount observed in 1908, the hope has been expressed that a period of immunity may be at hand. It hardly seems probable, however, that there is any periodicity in connection with the trouble. If there should be, it would overturn many expressed theories, relieve Bordeaux mixture, and the general practice of spraying from an obligation which in the minds of many men it now carries and lead investigation into other channels.

The conditions attending yellowing in cases of intermittent attacks, have been closely observed, and effort made to establish direct relation between these recurrent appearances and weather conditions, but without marked success. If the sudden appearance of many yellow leaves occurred repeatedly in connection with either wet or dry periods, this would be good evidence of causal relation to soil moisture, but such is not the case. One attack may come during a dry period, another in time of excessive moisture and still another when moisture conditions are normal, or, the several attacks of a season may all come at times when it is impossible to trace any relation to either shortage or excess of moisture. Of two contiguous orchards, apparently alike in soil and treatment, one may develop an abundance of yellow leaves at a time when the other has none. Occurrences of this nature tend rather to obscure than to make clear the true causes. In one case, an orchard, deeply cultivated, displayed an unusually large number of yellow leaves. Examination disclosed the fact that the cultivation had destroyed great quantities of feeding rootlets, enough to seriously affect the trees. That this disturbance of rootlets caused the outbreak of yellow leaves seems reasonable, but had only one portion of the orchard been so treated with the result of yellow leaves on that portion while there were none on the uncultivated portion, there would have been better basis for a definite conclusion. However, orchards in the neighborhood, that were not cultivated did not at this time develop yellow leaves. The fact that a considerable number of well sprayed orchards have been more or less seriously affected with yellowing of leaves has served as basis for an opinion, current among orchard owners, that Bordeaux mixture is responsible for the trouble. This often expressed opinion has been one of the factors determining the character of experiments undertaken by the Station. These experiments have been numerous and some of them are not yet concluded. From the work thus far done, it may be stated, that no conclusive evidence has been secured, indicating Bordeaux mixture as a cause of yellowing. Results for the last two seasons were negative, because of the almost entire absence of yellowing. In 1906, a few of the trees on plats sprayed with well made Bordeaux mixture, lost each a few leaves by yellowing, but the number was insignificant, and as the control trees lost much greater numbers, at the same time, it appears that the action of the Bordeaux was rather in the direction of retarding or checking than in promoting the trouble. In one instance, in 1905, a portion of an orchard sprayed by the department, was entirely free from yellow leaves, while adjoining portions sprayed at the same time by the owner, were seriously affected. Bordeaux mixture was used by both; that used by Station men was properly prepared; that used by the owner was neither well made nor well applied. There was gross carelessness at every stage of the process and the unfortunate results were not unexpected.

In one orchard under observation three spring applications of Bordeaux were made; the last on May 23. The foliage, except for a few brown spots on some of the leaves, was perfectly healthy until June 28, on which date yellow leaves began to appear. These increased in number, and July 1, were recorded as numerous on Whitney, Oldenburg, Grimes Golden, and especially on two trees of Sweet Belleflower. Ben Davis and Winesap had yellow leaves in much smaller numbers, very few on each tree. Light rains fell on July 1 and 2, a heavier one, followed by a strong wind, on the evening of July 3. July 4, all yellow leaves had fallen from the trees, and no more were seen until late in the month and then only a few. At the time of this attack of yellowing, apple trees in the neighborhood that had not yet been sprayed had as many yellow leaves as had the sprayed trees referred to, and certain ornamental and forest trees lost many leaves in the same way, and apparently from the same cause. Yellow leaves were particularly abundant on certain black cherry trees, while other trees of the same species were free from them. Tulip tree, basswood, sycamore, and elm trees were also observed to have many yellow leaves, all of which fell at the same time as the yellow apple leaves. In view of these observations, it is difficult to assign any connection between the spraying done in spring and the yellow leaves appearing in June.

While no direct and positive connection could be established between spraying with Bordeaux mixture and the yellowing of leaves, results with copper sulphate solution were quite different. Very good evidence was obtained showing that simple solutions of the copper salt do cause yellowing. A plat of eight trees was sprayed with a solution of copper sulphate 1:100 in June, following three spring applications of the Bordeaux-Paris green mixture. Except for a few brown spots, the foliage was in excellent condition at the time of applying the solution. The day after spraying with the copper sulphate almost every leaf was more or less brown spotted, and the green parts of many leaves exhibited that lighter shade of green which precedes yellowing. The next day yellowing was well advanced and leaves began falling. By the fourth day, the ground was covered with yellow leaves, and many more were falling. It was estimated that more than half the leaves became yellow and fell. A possible relation between brown spotting and yellowing is suggested in the fact that all yellow leaves had also brown spots. From under one tree, 1000 yellow leaves were gathered and examined. Every one was more or less brown spotted. Many leaves on the same tree, that were marked with brown spots, did not become yellow, and no relation could be traced between yellowing and the amount of brown spotting on individual leaves. Leaves having only one or two small brown spots became yellow as often, as did those in which half the area was brown.

On a second plat sprayed at the same time with a solution of half the strength, 1:200, some leaves became yellow, but probably not more than one fourth as many as on the plat treated with the stronger solution. There was also a great diminution in the amount of brown spotting, following use of the weaker solution. Adjoining plats, which received only the three earlier applications of Bordeaux mixture and Paris green were free from yellow leaves.

As a supplement to the work on these plats sprayed with solutions of copper sulphate and as a means of obtaining more detailed information, a number of small branches were diagramed, treated with the same solutions and examined daily for the development of injury. There was no regularity in the results obtained. In all cases, the first evidence of injury was seen in brown spots. Sometimes these spots appeared very soon after spraying and sometimes not for several days. They varied in number on individual leaves, and were of all sizes. Some leaves went thru the stages of yellowing and dropped off, but the number thus affected was not excessive. Grouping those branches treated with solutions, 1:200 and 1:100, the loss from yellowing was found to be 25 percent; with solutions 1:300 and 1:500 the loss was 15¾ percent.

Increase in strength of the solution increased the amount of brown spotting much more rapidly than it increased the yellowing of leaves.

COPPER NOT ABSORBED THRU BARK OF TRUNK AND BRANCHES

In spraying with Bordeaux mixture, the trunks and branches of trees become thoroly coated, and this coating is persistently held for long periods. This fact undoubtedly suggested a question which has been frequently asked, namely—"Is copper sulphate absorbed thru the bark in sufficient quantity to cause yellowing of leaves"? The outer corky layer of the bark of trees is extremely resistant to all destructive agencies and is regarded as quite impermeable to water or other liquids. It does not seem probable that Bordeaux mixture, or copper sulphate solution, could exert any injurious influence on leaves thru this channel, but in order to test the matter in a somewhat definite way, it was arranged to maintain liquids in contact with the bark, for a considerable time and observe results.

Upright branches were chosen, whose laterals could be brought, by means of bandages, within the limits of the bore of a 2½ inch rubber tube. A piece of tubing, 15 inches long, was then slipped down the branch and the lower end tied tightly, so that no liquid could escape. The tube was then filled with liquid, which was replenished as often as was necessary to keep the tube full. Four tubes were prepared. Number 1 filled with copper sulphate solution 1:100; number 2 with copper sulphate solution, 1:500; number 3 with standard Bordeaux mixture, and number 4, with distilled water. Examination was made daily for more than a month. No injury of any kind could be detected and the test was then discontinued. The bark appears to be impervious to the liquids tested.

Copper Sulphate Solution Absorbed Thru Wounds

The tubes were now adjusted to other branches and filled with the same liquids freshly prepared. Within the tubes, and in such position as to be emersed in the liquids, small notches were cut thru the bark into the alburnun. The precipitate of Bordeaux mixture, as was expected, prevented absorption thru the cut, and this tube was soon discontinued. Distilled water was taken in freely, without any injurious effect. The two copper sulphate solutions were also absorbed thru the cut in considerable quantity. These tubes were filled at 11:15 a. m. July 5. At 5:00 p. m. of the same day the effect of the stronger solution, 1:100, was apparent in a brown discoloration which was confined to the midribs and their branches. No effect from the weaker solution, 1:500, could be detected at this time. When examined at 9:00 a. m. July 6, browning could be detected in all leaves above the point of attachment on both branches. Browning was in a much more advanced stage on the branch supplied with the stronger solution than on that supplied with the weaker solution. Many leaves were entirely browned and some of these were variously curled. As the injury spread from the vascular bundles the tips and margins of the leaves were browned first. The last portions to lose the green color were longitudinal strips on either side of the midrib. The morning of July 7 the effect of the solutions, on leaves of branches below the attachment began to appear. The injury extended gradually and irregularly as regards the order in which lateral branches were affected until July 20 when observations were discontinued. The stronger solution had extended its influence a little farther than the weaker; otherwise there were no differences in the results. There was at no time any evidence of yellowing. The affected leaves all became brown. They died and were more or less curled. Some persisted and some fell. This experiment was repeated several times and always with the same result.

Attachment of the tube as described above is shown in Figure 1. This illustration is from a photograph of a branch of Whitney apple used in one of the later experiments. The branch as shown has a length of about 12 feet. The lateral to which the tube is adjusted is nearly central. The solution as absorbed killed the leaves on this lateral first, then extended its influence to the main branch. In about a week all leaves on the branch photographed were dead and many had fallen. A solution of copper sulphate 1:500 was used. Attachment was made at 9 a. m. August 1. At 6 p. m. the same day no injurious effect was apparent, but at 8 a. m. August 2 all but 26 of the 245 leaves on the lateral above the tube were more or less browned. Extension of injury to other laterals was gradual and irregular.

Following this same line of work, copper sulphate solutions, of varying degrees of concentration, were introduced into four and five year old trees by siphon attachment to roots. It is not the intention to discuss these experiments in detail at this time, but it may be stated that in all cases injury resulted in the form of browning of leaves. In

FIG. 1. Copper sulphate solution 1:500 absorbed thru wound within the tube killed all the leaves on this branch. From photograph August 8, 1906.

no case did yellowing of leaves follow absorption of solutions thru the roots. The time of appearance and rate of development of injury bore a distinct relation to the strength of the solution used, but it was always the same kind of injury, a browning or burning of the leaves.

Up to this time the solutions used varied between 1:100 and 1:1000 and all produced browning of leaves with no symptoms of yellowing. It was then thought desirable to ascertain the limit of dilution that would cause browning, the quantity of solution required, the time necessary to give first evidence of injury, and the point in dilution, if such existed, that would effect just the degree of injury that would result in yellowing instead of in the total browning of the leaves. During July and August 1908 a series of 21 experiments was carried out. The results obtained, while very interesting and suggestive, are not conclusive and this work will be extended the present season.

INJECTION OF COPPER SULPHATE SOLUTION 1:25000 FOLLOWED BY YELLOWING OF LEAVES

For the present, brief mention of the results from one tree (Number 14) may be given. A bottle with capacity for holding 4 litres of the solution was supported about 6 feet above the ground and connected by a glass siphon with a hole bored into the alburnum about 1 foot above the ground. This connection was thru a rubber cork, so adjusted that no liquid could escape. The accompanying Figure 2 shows this tree and the manner of attachment. Graduations were arranged on the outside of the bottle in such manner that readings could be made of the approximate amounts of solution absorbed within a given time.

Copper sulphate solution 1:25,000 was used for this tree. The connection was made at 2:00 p. m. August 31. Between 2:00 p. m. and 6:00 p. m. 3.3 litres of solution passed into the tree. From 6:00 p. m. August 31 to 8:00 a. m. September 1 the amount taken in was 1.4 litres; from 8:00 a. m. to 3:00 p. m. September 1, 1.8 litres; from 3:00 p. m. September 1 to 8:00 a. m. September 2, 1.05 litres. From this time the amounts absorbed grew smaller until work with the tree was discontinued October 3.

The total amount of solution taken in by the tree in 33 days was 18.33 litres. The first injurious effect was observed on the morning of September 4, ninety hours after the attachment was made. The tree had at that time absorbed 9.6 litres of solution. The injury, as first seen, consisted in a discoloration of the vascular system in a few of the lower leaves on a branch directly above the point where the solution entered. This browning was visible, at first, only by looking thru the leaves, but a few hours later it had spread and produced the characteristic surface appearance. The morning of September 5 these leaves were completely brown; they numbered about 20. No further spread of this injury occurred. September 13 some of the leaves above, on the same branch carrying the browned leaves, exhibited yellow spots which gradually enlarged and, on the morning of September 14 several leaves were entirely yellow and ready to fall, and were removed. Other leaves became affected in the same way and this continued until every leaf on the branch was removed. The two branches next above the one here considered, diverged at a considerable angle and were separated vertically by several inches. A

FIG. 2. Tree No. 14 supplied with solution of copper sulphate 1:25000. Yellowing
of leaves was produced on this tree. In 33 days the tree
absorbed 18.33 litres of solution.

few inches further up another branch projected almost immediately above the one whose leaves had fallen. September 20 lower leaves of this branch showed evidences of yellowing and the next day several were yellow. Other leaves on this branch became affected and, by October 3 about half the leaves borne by this branch had fallen. No other leaves, besides those on these two branches, were in any way affected, nor did yellow leaves appear on other trees at this time. It appears that the yellowing of leaves on this tree was caused by the copper sulphate solution absorbed, but the manner in which the injury was produced remains for future investigation. Of the leaves that became yellow, 97 were collected and subjected to analysis. They contained 8.2 milligrams of copper sulphate, showing quite conclusively that the copper penetrated to the leaves. The results obtained from this tree and from others in the series indicate possible correlation between strength of solution and amount of copper absorbed on the one hand, and kind and degree of injury on the other. They encourage continuance of this line of investigation which was stopped by the lateness of the season.

THE RELATION OF METEORIC WATERS TO FOLIAGE INJURY

COVERED AND UNCOVERED TREES

The opinion has been frequently expressed that injuries to leaves, following the applications of Bordeaux mixture, have direct relation to atmospheric conditions. This view is based upon the observation that brown spotting, more or less severe, often follows applications made during wet weather, or, may suddenly appear following rain that is defered anywhere from one to six weeks or longer. Some of the reported cases of injuries that appear to be directly connected with rainfall present anomalies not readily explained, for example, trees well coated with Bordeaux mixture, may be washed by rains at intervals of several days and no injury to foliage appears; then another rain falls, and, immediately after, serious injury occurs. A case in point happened in our station work in an orchard in the western part of the state. The fact of injury, immediately following a particular rain, naturally suggests that rain as the immediate cause, but why did not earlier rains have the same effect? Was there some particular quality in or condition attendant on this rain that gave it a power for injury that the other rains did not have? These are questions difficult to answer because of incomplete records. The injury comes unexpectedly. It is well developed when discovered and the restrospective enumeration of conditions just preceding is likely to miss the important factor, and thus attach an element of uncertainty to any conclusion that may be reached. Various suggestions have been offered to account for the injurious action of some rains, as contrasted with the harmlessness of others. A rain is injurious because the waters hold in solution an unusual amount of carbon dioxide which exerts its solvent action upon the copper compounds on the leaves and this copper in solution effects the injury. An electrical condition of the atmosphere operates upon the copper, and, aided by the water brings an injurious amount into solution. The carbon dioxide of the air, in the days preceding the rain, converted sufficient copper on the leaves to soluble form so that only moisture was needed to effect the injury. These and other like conjectures have no tangible basis; they are questions difficult to prove for particular cases, and equally difficult to disprove. But while uncertainty may attend the exact manner in which injuries are effected it must be accepted as fact that meteoric waters do play an important part. Other atmospheric conditions, temperature, humidity, electrical conditions, wind, clouds, and sunshine may one or all have influence at times and contribute to the effects observed, but dew, and rain, especially the latter, must be regarded as the most active agents in those cases of injury that occur in spite of all precautions taken to avoid them. While this conclusion is based upon a considerable number of reports of conditions attending particular cases of injury and upon many field observations, it seemed advisable to test the matter in a more detailed manner. To this end two four year old apple trees growing five feet apart in rows ten feet apart were selected and given the numbers 26 and 27 in the regular series of numbers for the season of 1906. These trees were of about equal size and form as indicated by the following measurements:

	26	27
Total height June 28	5 feet 5 inches	5 feet 2 inches
Diameter at the ground	1⅝ inches	1¾ inches
Ground to first branches	3 feet 3 inches	3 feet 2 inches
Spread	2 feet	1 foot 9 inches

During the season tree Number 26 added 1 foot 1 inch to its height and 1 foot 8 inches to its spread while tree Number 27 increased 1 foot in height and 7 inches in spread. The trees had received one application of Bordeaux mixture and Paris green at the time of the regular spraying in April, but at the commencement of this test no traces of the early application could be found. The leaves on both trees were dark green, healthy in appearance and very free from injuries of any kind. On the morning of June 28 the trees were sprayed alike with Bordeaux mixture, carefully made, after the 4–4–50 formula. Each tree received three applications, allowing time to thoroly dry between applications. When dry after the third application both trees presented a very blue appearance; the leaves were thoroly coated. From this time until October 13, a period of 107 days, tree No. 26 was exposed to all atmospheric conditions, while tree No. 27 was protected from dew and rain. This protection was secured by means of a houselike structure so adjusted that it could be drawn over the tree at evening or at any time when rain threatened. The cover in position and the uncovered companion tree, at the left, as photographed July 4, 1906 are shown in Figure 3.

Full exposure was allowed every day except when there was immediate prospect of rain. During the period there were seven full days and several half days when the cover remained on because of rain. No rain fell on the remaining days of June. During July rain fell on 11 days. The amounts were small except on two days—0.6 inch July 12 and 0.55 inch July 23. The total for the month was 2.17 inches. Both trees were critically examined July 20 and it was then plainly evident that the rain, up to that time amounting to 1.61 inches, together with the possible aid of the frequent heavy dews, had considerably reduced the amount of Bordeaux upon the leaves of the exposed tree, while the protected tree was to all appearances as well coated as on the day when sprayed. On the exposed tree 5 leaves were yellow and a considerable number were marked by

FIG. 3.   Two trees sprayed alike June 28.   The one on the left exposed.   The one on the right protected from rain and dew until October 13, a period of 107 days.

brown tips, small circular spots or brown marginal areas. These injuries individually were small and, as the majority of leaves were uninjured, the entire injury, while noticeable, was not regarded as serious. On the protected tree no leaves were injured.

During August the rainfall was nearly twice as heavy as for July. Rain fell on 12 days giving a total precipitation of 4.2 inches. The heaviest rain of the season fell during the night of August 17 when the gauge indicated 1.93 inches; this was followed by showers on August 18 and 19 bringing the precipitation for the 3 days to 2.54 inches. This heavy rain had a marked effect upon the exposed tree in removing Bordeaux 'from the leaves. The tree lost its blue color and returned to normal green which appeared in strong contrast with the decided blue of the covered tree. The yellow leaves, noted as present on the exposed tree on July 20, fell during rain July 28, and no further yellowing occurred until August 11, on which date a few were noted. A few days later, August 14, a few leaves, mainly small basal leaves ón small spurs on the protected tree exhibited the lighter greenish yellow color that indicated eventual yellowing and death for these leaves. On the únprotected tree there was, at this time, an evident increase in number of yellow leaves. August 17 the yellow leaves were removed by hand from both trees; there were 55 from the unprotected tree and 18 from the protected tree. On the unprotected tree the yellow leaves were distributed over the tree; many of them being full' sized leaves on terminal shoots; while those from the protected tree were almost entirely small leaves from the bases of short spurs. The number of leaves removed, cannot be taken as representing the total number of leaves turning yellow on the two trees, because it is probable that some fell and were blown away between August 11, when yellowing was first noticed, and the date of removal of those remaining, but the numbers represent very well the relative yellowing on the two trees. This appearance of yellow leaves on these two trees was not coincident with any epidemic of the same trouble upon other trees of this and other plats. The orchards were at this time practically free from yellow leaves. The cause may then be regarded as local in the affected trees or in their treatment.

About the middle of August the ravages of an insect pest began to show conspicuously on the leaves of the unprotected tree. This insect, the apple leaf skeletonizer, was unusually abundant this season. Attacking the leaves as it does in late summer, after the protective influence of the early commercial spray has been largely removed by rains, it does serious injury, particularly to young trees. The coating of Bordeaux mixture present on the leaves of the tree protected from rain was sufficient, altho containing no arsenites, to ward off attacks of this insect and there was no injury except on a few of the leaves that unfolded after the spraying was done, and hence had no protective covering. The unprotected tree, from the leaves of which the Bordeaux mixture had been mostly removed by rain, had so many leaves entirely destroyed and so many others badly injured that the general appearance of the tree was changed; the foliage appeared scant, curled, brown, and in general, unsightly. This served to heighten the contrast between the two trees.

Rain to the amount of 2.39 inches fell on 8 days in September and there was one light rain of 0.14 inch in October before the test with these trees was discontinued.

For the period during which the test was carried on, June 28 to October 13, 107 days, the total rainfall to which tree No. 26 was exposed and from which tree No. 27 was protected was 8.9 inches. As already remarked, the blue color imparted to the leaves by the Bordeaux mixture disappeared from tree No. 26 with the rains of August 17–19, but some leaves retained small spots of the mixture to the end. These spots would not be noticed in casual examination, but could be found by close inspection of individual leaves. The foliage of tree No. 27 kept dry during this period of 107 days was still blue October 13, but not of so intense a blue as had existed immediately after spraying. It is probable that some of the Bordeaux became loosened and fell as dry flakes when leaves were rubbed together by wind; the blue color was also toned down by accumulations of dust which settled upon the leaves, still the leaves were, on the final date, October 13, conspicuously well coated and blue in color.

All leaves on both trees were picked October 13; the number from tree No. 26 was 1106, from tree No. 27, 1506; the difference of 400 between the two trees does not mean that tree No. 27 had originally a greater number of leaves than tree No. 26, but may be interpreted as showing that the combined action of the skeletonizer, rain and wind caused the fall of a greater number of leaves from tree No. 26 than did the action of wind alone upon tree No. 27.

In 1907 this test was repeated on the same trees beginning June 10 and ending November 7, making the period 150 days. The season up to September 1, covering more than half the period of the test, was extremely wet; the latter part of the period was rather dry or with only moderate rains. During the test of the preceding year the exposed tree was subjected to a total of 27 rains and there were 6 additional days on which there were traces of rain. For 1907 this tree was exposed to 46 rains and there were 16 days on which there were traces of rain. The precipitation for the period was 14.88 inches and more than three-fourths of this fell before September 1. The trees as they appeared October 17, 1907, are shown in figure 4.

One notable difference between the two tests was the greater adhesiveness of the Bordeaux on the exposed tree in 1907 as compared with 1906. The heavy rains of July and August, 1907, reduced the blue color of the leaves somewhat, but on September 1 trunk and branches were still very blue; some leaves had a full coating and nearly all other leaves bore conspicuous blue patches. Later rains did not greatly reduce the amount adhering and, when the leaves were gathered November 7, a large proportion of them still retained considerable Bordeaux mixture. It is not thought probable that the difference in adhesiveness can be ascribed to differences in the rains to which the tree was subjected, but is more likely due to differences in the lime used in making the mixture. There is no definite data on this point at hand, but in other experiments it has been found that character of the lime has a marked influence on adhesiveness and that two lots of the same brand, both equally fresh and not at all air-slaked, may give mixtures that are unequal in a marked degree in the matter of adhesiveness.

Leaves of the covered tree remained free from injury thruout the season and except for the dullness of color due to accumulated dust were as blue when picked as in the first days following the applications June 10. No yellowing of leaves appeared on either tree, but leaves of the exposed tree were marked by brown spots and marginal areas to about the same extent as were those from the same

FIG. 4. Two trees sprayed alike June 10, 1907. The tree on the left exposed. The tree on the right protected from rain and dew until November 7, a period of 150 days.

tree in the preceding year. Again, for the third time this test was repeated in 1908. This time on two trees in another plat, and under abnormally dry conditions. The precipitation for the full period of the test was 6.36 inches, less than half the amount for the preceding year. Results, as far as action on foliage is concerned, were essentially the same as for the other trials.

The uniformity of the results obtained under the widely different conditions which characterized the three seasons, fully establish the importance of meteoric waters in their relation to injury to foliage following applications of Bordeaux mixture. In no case was there any appearance of injury on leaves of the protected trees, while in each test the foliage of the tree exposed to rain was in some degree injured. The utmost care was taken in the preparation of the mixtures, applications were the same for the trees compared and all conditions were equal except in the one matter, that in each test one tree was protected from rain and dew. Injuries to foliage of the exposed trees were not very serious, and yet, an aggregate of the dead leaf areas must have reduced the working leaf surface to an appreciable and undesirable extent. By no means all leaves were affected; often of two contiguous leaves, one would be perfectly healthy while its neighbor was dead at the tip or had long narrow strips of dead tissue along the margin or was more or less disfigured by circular or irregular brown areas of varying size, distributed over the surface. Why one of two neighboring leaves, apparently exactly alike and having the same exposure, should be injured and the other not affected is an unanswered question. A suggested inequality in composition and distribution of the mixture is not an acceptable explanation, because agitation before and during the process of spraying was so thoro that composition must have been uniform. It is certainly not a question of quantity, because of two leaves the injured may show a decidedly less amount of Bordeaux upon its surface than the uninjured. Slight structural differences, or varying degrees of vitality might be assumed to account for differences in liability to injury but there is no proof of the existence of such differences and the question remains open for further investigation.

CHANGES OCCURRING IN BORDEAUX MIXTURE

If attention is given to the selection of materials, and if these materials are brought together in proper proportions in accordance with standard formulas, no copper remains in the clear supernatant liquid, as the precipitate subsides. In this fact we have evidence that the copper has all been converted into insoluble compounds and the Bordeaux mixture rendered safe for application to foliage. If the mixture is allowed to stand, changes take place. These changes may occur more or less promptly, according to the quality and quantity of lime present and are first apparent in the color of the mixture. The bright sky blue characteristic of well made Bordeaux becomes darker, greenish shades appear and finally the precipitate assumes and retains a dingy purple color. The chemical transpositions that occur have not been determined, but it is known that some of the copper becomes soluble and that for this reason mixtures that have stood for some time are not safe to apply. Color appears to be a guide that can be depended upon. As long as the original blue is retained there appears to be no difference in the effect upon foliage between perfectly fresh mixture and that which has stood for a week or more. However, it is the common practice to use only fresh made mixtures, both because they are safer and usually most convenient.

If changes occur in Bordeaux mixture in mass, it is reasonable to believe that similar or possibly much more radical changes will occur when the mixture is sprayed upon foliage and thus spread out with maximum exposure to the air and the elements. The color changes frequently observed in mixtures in bulk do not usually appear in mixtures thinly spread on foliage; the original blue is retained thruout the season or as long as the coating remains on the leaves. Sometimes burning of the leaves follows immediately upon application, in other cases like injury may appear after a delay of several days or even several weeks; degree of injury may vary from slight to the nearly complete defoliation of the trees; and again no injury that can in any way be connected with the mixture occurs, the leaves remain in perfectly healthy condition and perform their functions to the normal end of the season.

The Problem of Solubility of the Copper of Bordeaux Mixture on Leaves

Early in this investigation of injuries to foliage by materials applied in spraying, repeated tests were made of the separate ingredients of Bordeaux mixture. Trees were sprayed heavily with milk of lime of varying degrees of concentration and to other trees solutions of copper sulphate in varying degrees of dilution were applied. In no case was any injury inflicted by milk of lime, but it was clearly demonstrated that injury promptly followed the application of even very dilute solutions of copper sulphate. These injuries are of the same character as those that follow spraying with Bordeaux mixture. It is therefore concluded that the copper in solution is the active agent responsible for the burning of foliage. Numerous tests show that fresh and rightly made Bordeaux mixture contains no soluble copper. We must then conclude that changes take place in Bordeaux mixture after deposition on the leaves, and that copper becomes soluble, at least in some cases, in sufficient quantity to effect injury. Numerous observations made in the field, and critical study of particular cases of injury, have suggested several questions, answers to which are necessary to an understanding of the anomalous and often contradictory results following field experiments in the application of Bordeaux mixtures. How soon after deposition on the leaves does soluble copper appear? Thru what agencies does copper become soluble? Does absence of injury mean absence of copper in solution? Is appearance of injury synchronous with appearance of soluble copper? Does the presence of lime in excess prevent or retard solubility of copper? Is the view expressed by Millardet and Gayon, that copper remains in insoluble form until all free lime has been neutralized or washed away, correct? With what degree of rapidity is excess lime removed? Does the appearance of injury correlate with entire removal of free lime? A considerable number of experiments have been conducted for the purpose of finding answers to these and other questions of like nature, and we may now consider a portion of these experiments in some detail.

It is a currently expressed opinion that the insoluble copper compounds deposited on the leaves in Bordeaux mixtures are acted upon by the carbon dioxide of the air and by the carbon dioxide, ammonia, and nitric acid contained in dew and rain waters and thru these agencies converted into soluble forms which are then capable of working injury to the leaves.

Bordeaux Mixture in Glass Dishes

Following, in part, a test reported by Schander[1] 20 c.c. of Bordeaux mixture carefully made on the 4–4–50 formula and which contained no copper in solution was placed in each of 4 six inch crystallizing dishes on May 12. The dishes were given the numbers 16, 17, 18 and 19. Nos. 16 and 17 were placed in shade on a laboratory table, Nos. 18 and 19 in a south window as much exposed to the sun as possible. No. 17 in shade and No. 19 in sun were kept permanently dry. No. 16 in shade and No. 18 in sun were moistened with cistern water almost daily, or to be exact, 54 times in the 65 days to and including July 16. July 16, the dishes were placed in the hands of the chemists for examination of the contents and determination of the state of the copper as regards solubility. Below is the report submitted, with conclusions, by Dr. H. S. Grindley and Mr. O. S. Watkins.

Bordeaux Mixtures. Report upon Numbers 16–19, inclusive

Received July 16, 1906

Each of the residues in the crystallizing dishes was digested thoroly with cold neutral distilled water. The filtrates were very slightly alkaline to litmus paper but they were very slightly acid to phenolphthalein.

To make the filtrates neutral to phenolphthalein it took the following amounts of $^N/_{20}$ NaOH solution—No. 16, 0.35 c.c.; No. 17, 0.31 c.c.; No. 18, 0.40 c.c.; No. 19, 0.40 c.c.

The solutions before titration and after titration were perfectly colorless and therefore did not show any indication of copper.

The neutralized solutions were evaporated to a very small volume (5–10 c.c.). They were slightly acidified with a few drops of H_2SO_4 and then treated with hydrogen sulphide gas. No trace of a precipitate of copper sulphide appeared. Not even a dark coloration of the solution was produced. These filtrates were saved under the labels 16A, 17A, 18A, and 19A.

The residues remaining from the extracts with cold water were distinctly blue in color and they apparently consisted largely of insoluble copper salts. They were treated with a few c.c. of diluted nitric acid. They effervesced vigorously, showing much carbonic acid.

---
[1]Schander, R. Landw. Jahrb. 33 (1904), p. 522.

The residues readily and completely dissolved in the dilute nitric acid. The solutions thus resulting were saved with the labels Nos. 16B, 17B, 18B, and 19B.

Conclusions.—First by the action of the air or by the air and water used in moistening the Bordeaux mixtures no soluble copper salts were produced. At least after the action had continued from the 12th day of May to the present time, there was no soluble copper salts in either of the four cases.

Second, the strong akalinity due to the lime of the Bordeaux mixture had been completely neutralized by the action of the air and moisture. The lime and the copper had apparently been mostly converted into the carbonates of those metals.

Signed   H. S. GRINDLEY,

July 20, 1906.   O. S. WATKINS.

BORDEAUX MIXTURE ON FOLIAGE OF APPLE TREES IN POTS

In order to more nearly approximate the actual conditions to which Bordeaux mixture, as sprayed on foliage, is subjected, a further test of exposure to atmospheric conditions in a constantly dry condition and in an intermittently wet condition was made as follows:

Two one year old Northwestern Greening apple trees, growing in eight-inch pots, were sprayed at the same time and with the same Bordeaux mixture, freshly made after the 4–4–50 formula. The trees were sprayed three times, allowing intervals sufficient to thoroly dry the foliage between applications. When finally dried both trees were thoroly coated. The spraying was done on May 24, and the trees, to which the numbers 81 and 83 had been given were then placed side by side, on the sill of a south window. No. 83 was kept continually dry. No. 81 was sprayed with cistern water (delivered in a fine mist by means of an atomizer) on 46 of the 54 days of the period from May 24 to July 17. In these applications of water, the amount was regulated to simply moisten the Bordeaux upon the leaves, without causing any removal of material by dripping. July 17 the the trees were given to the chemists and report of the examination for soluble copper is given herewith:

REPORT ON FOLIAGE INJURY WORK. NOS. 20 AND 21
Received July 17, 1906

The leaves and small stems of tree No. 81 were washed as free as possible from the Bordeaux mixture with neutral distilled water. After drying, the leaves of the tree showed a white residue still remaining (probably a mixture of $CaCO_3$ and $CaSO_4$), but scarcely any of the blue residue of the copper salt.

The residue washed off the leaves with the water was removed from the latter by filtration which gave a clear, colorless filtrate and a green colored residue. The residue was dissolved in dilute nitric acid and saved under the label No. 81b. The treatment with acid caused the evolution of CO_2 in considerable quantity.

The filtrate was very slightly alkaline to litmus, but very slightly acid to phenolphthalein. It required 0.75 c.c. N/10 KOH to make the solution neutral to phenolphthalein.

The solution was labelled 81a, evaporated to a small volume and tested for soluble copper compounds by treating with hydrogen sulphide. An excess of hydrogen sulphide gave no precipitate. The solution was not even darkened by the H_2S. This proves that no soluble copper salts were present.

The leaves and small stems of tree No. 83 were washed with neutral distilled water as well as possible. After drying, the leaves showed practically the same coating as described above for tree No. 81.

The residue washed off the leaves was separated and treated as described above in the case of tree No. 81. The residue insoluble in water was dissolved in dilute nitric acid and saved under the label No. 83b. The addition of the nitric acid caused considerable CO_2 to be evolved.

The filtrate was very slightly alkaline to litmus, but very slightly acid to phenolphthalein. It required 0.75 c.c. N/10 KOH to make the solution neutral to phenolphthalein. The solution was labeled 83a evaporated to a small volume and tested for soluble copper compounds by treating it with hydrogen sulphide. The excess of hydrogen sulphide gave no precipitate. The solution was not even darkened by the H_2S. This proves that no soluble copper salts were present.

Conclusions

First, by washing the leaves of these trees with neutral distilled water no unchanged lime or calcium hydroxide was removed by the process. That is, apparently, the alkalinity of the original Bordeaux mixture due to the excess of lime used in making it, was either neutralized by the CO_2 of the air, or by the acid constituents upon the surface of the leaves, or the lime was washed out by the water if the latter was used in sufficient quantity to run or drip off the leaves.

Second, by washing the leaves of these trees with neutral distilled water no soluble copper salts were removed.

Third, the insoluble greenish-blue residue washed from the leaves dissolved readily in dilute nitric acid and it contained considerable carbon dioxide in the form of a carbonate. By the washing considerable quantities of insoluble copper compounds were removed from the leaves.

Fourth, no differences in any respects could be observed between the solutions or the insoluble residues washed off from the two trees.

Signed   H. S. GRINDLEY.

July 24, 1906.

The results of these two experiments exactly coincide. In neither case was copper in solution detected. The Bordeaux remaining in glass dishes for 65 days in full exposure to the air, and whether kept dry or intermittently wet, did not have any of its copper converted to soluble form, but did have all of its excess calcium oxide rendered inert. Likewise, in the case of the sprayed trees, no copper became soluble, but the lime was all changed to insoluble form. It should be stated in regard to the trees that all leaves were thoroly coated with the Bordeaux mixture, that there was no apparent diminution of the blue color and that no burning or brown-spotting occurred.

FIELD EXPERIMENTS WITH SPRAYED TREES IN 1906.

While these experiments, which were carried on in the laboratory, were in progress, plans were made for certain other field experiments designed to supplement the laboratory series and to answer some questions which those experiments were not calculated to reach. Information was particularly desired regarding the conditions under which and the time when soluble copper first appeared, the rapidity with which it became soluble and the relation between the appearance of copper and injuries to leaves. It was also deemed important that an attempt be made to correlate weather conditions and any changes that took place in the Bordeaux spread upon the leaves. It was, therefore, arranged to equip certain four year old apple trees, growing in the department plats, with appliances for catching and holding rain or spray waters passing over the leaves and then subjecting the waters collected to chemical analysis, for determination of alkalinity, soluble copper and arsenic. The trees chosen were those that, from location, size and form of crown, seemed best adapted for the purpose.

Each tree was supplied with a ring made of quarter inch, round, galvanized iron, forty inches in diameter. This ring was supported, above the greatest spread of the tree, at a height between five and six feet, by four wooden posts, so braced as to prevent any displacement by wind. From this ring a funnel, made of a heavy grade of table oil-cloth, was suspended and so adjusted about the trunk of the tree that no water could escape except thru the mouth of the funnel, which was arranged to open into a five gallon jar supported in proper position. The arrangement as described was then surrounded with a bur-lap curtain, to prevent rain from driving against the outside of the funnel and dripping into the jar.

Five trees, designated by the numbers 33, 34, 35 and 36 and 49 were thus equipped during the summer of 1906.

TREE NUMBER 33

The preliminary spray was applied to tree No. 33 July 21. For this spray the mixture in most common use in the commercial orchards of the state was used. The formula is as follows:

Copper sulphate	4 pounds
Fresh slaked lime	4 pounds
Paris green	¼ pound
Water	50 gallons

The tree was sprayed three times allowing intervals sufficient for thoro drying between applications. When spraying was completed, the tree was thoroly coated. The funnel was then adjusted and the tree left exposed to the sun and to any rains that might fall. July 28, seven days after spraying, the first rain came as a thunder shower with precipitation amounting to 0.55 inch. The water falling within the ring, most of which passed over the sprayed leaves to the jar below, measured 11.28 litres (approximately three gallons). This water was taken to the chemical laboratory, filtered, a sample taken for determination of alkalinity, the balance concentrated by evaporation and stored for subsequent determination of copper and arsenic. The residue, left on filtering, and which was seen to contain many small flakes and particles of insoluble Bordeaux, was also preserved for determination of the insoluble copper. Other rains followed at intervals of from one to nine days until October 13, on which date the leaves remaining were picked and work with the tree discontinued. During the period of 84 days from July 21 to October 13 the tree was subjected to the waters of twenty-one rains, varying in amount from 0.01 inch to 1.93 inches, and which classify as—thunder storms 7; light local showers 11; protracted rains 3. The total precipitation was 7.30 inches. The 21 lots of water collected ranged from 304 c.c. to 20,191 c.c.; from less than one pint to more than five gallons. The aggregate was a little more than 33 gallons. To this should be added about five gallons, making the total water falling within the ring approximately 38 gallons. This addition is explained by the fact that the heaviest rain (1.93 inches August 17) came during the night, and the amount falling within the ring exceeded the capacity of the jar, so that a quantity, computed from the ratios of other rains at about five gallons was lost.

The spray applied to this tree was much in excess of applications made in common orchard practice; leaves and branches were thoroly coated and were uniformly of a Bordeaux blue color. Notwithstanding the heavy application, injury to foliage was extremely small. Two days after the rain of July 28, that is to say, nine days after spraying, a very slight browning on the margins of a few leaves was observed. This injury was neither conspicuous, nor in any way serious. Two weeks later, immediately following the showers of August 10 a few small brown spots were noted on a few of the leaves. During the season a few leaves became yellow and fell; these were mainly the small basal leaves of clusters. This yellowing can not be ascribed to any effect of the spray for the reason that, at the same time, a somewhat larger number of yellow leaves was observed on similar trees that had not been sprayed. On completion of the chemical analyses the results were brought together as shown in the tabulation page 255.

The significant feature of the results, as tabulated, is the early and continuous appearance of soluble copper. An appreciable quantity— 16.5 milligrams per litre—was present in the waters from the rain which fell seven days after spraying. With the exception of the second rain, the amount of water from which was very small, measureable amounts of copper were determined from the waters of all following rains. The amount varied between 8.9 milligrams and 85 milligrams per litre. There is marked irregularity in the amounts of copper indicated and no definite relation can be traced between these amounts and, either intervals of time, or character of the storms. In some cases it appears that small amounts of drip waters give proportionately larger quantities of copper than do the larger amounts, but this does not hold for all cases. No satisfactory reason has been found to account for such fluctuations as appear between waters from the rains of September 19 to September 27. After a time interval of 7 days a local shower with precipitation of 0.09 inch giving 1.7 litres of drip, yields copper to the amount of 56.1 milligrams per litre; then following an interval of $3\frac{1}{4}$ days another local shower of 0.43 inch and 9 litres of drip gives 22.2 milligrams per litre; next, after the same interval a light shower measuring 0.03 of an inch and giving 0.9 litre of water shows 84.9 milligrams of soluble copper per litre, and following

Chemical Determinations from Waters Collected from Tree Number 33.

Serial number	Date	Amount of drip	Soluble constituents of drip waters					Sediment filtered from drip waters			
			Copper		Alkalinity in terms of calcium oxide		Arsenic in terms of As$_2$O$_3$	Insoluble copper		Insoluble arsenic	
			Total Milligrams	Milligrams Per litre	Total Milligrams	Milligrams Per litre		Total Milligrams	Milligrams Per litre	Total Milligrams	Milligrams Per litre
3	July 29	12.23	202.0	16.5	105.8	8.6	1.5	773.6	6.3	121.5	9.9
3 b	July 30	.31	Trace	....	Trace	...	None	Trace	.....	Trace	....
3 c	August 5	2.32	87.2	37.5	10.5	4.5	Trace	301.6	13.0	24.1	10.3
3 e	August 7	1.25	42.4	33.9	4.1	3.2	Trace	103.6	82.8	20.1	16.0
3 f	August 8	5.73	57.2	9.9	33.7	5.8	Trace	390.4	68.1	33.4	5.8
3 g	August 9	1.40	19.6	14.0	5.8	4.1	Trace	349.2	249.4	20.6	14.4
3 h	August 10	7.18	64.0	8.9	47.1	6.5	1.0	398.8	55.5	39.0	5.4
3 i	August 18	20.90	696.0	33.3	87.2	4.1	2.0	291.2	13.9	12.6	0.6
3 j	August 18	3.55	32.4	9.1	18.3	5.1	Trace	174.8	49.2	10.4	2.9
3 k	August 19	8.67	94.4	10.8	26.5	3.0	Trace	389.6	45.1	19.7	2.2
3 l	August 24	1.50	22.8	15.2	1.3	0.8	Trace	104.4	69.6	Trace	....
3 n	August 26	14.80	154.0	10.4	14.5	0.9	Trace	337.2	22.7	27.4	1.8
3 o	Sept. 3	1.25	15.2	12.1	Too dark	...	0.90	70.4	56.3	10.5	8.4
3 p	Sept. 12	1.77	75.6	42.7	Too dark	...	0.50	61.6	34.8	Trace	....
3 q	Sept. 19	1.70	95.4	56.1	Too dark	...	Trace	300.8	176.9	13.7	8.0
3 r	Sept. 22	9.00	200.0	22.2	Neutral	...	0.70	348.8	38.7	24.2	2.7
3 s	Sept. 26	0.90	76.4	84.9	Too dark	...	Trace	40.4	44.9	Trace	....
3 t	Sept. 27	5.72	80.0	13.9	Too dark	...	Trace	130.8	22.8	10.7	1.8
3 u	Sept. 29	10.51	204.4	19.4	Neutral	...	0.8	275.6	26.2	19.8	1.8
3 v	October 1	17.26	207.2	11.8	Neutral	...	1.0	217.2	12.6	21.4	1.2
3 w	October 4	2.28	72.4	31.7	Too dark	...	Trace	121.6	53.3	9.7	4.2

this in 12 hours another shower precipitating 0.27 inch and yielding 5.72 litres of water gives 13.9 milligrams of copper per litre.

Alkalinity decreases until neutrality is reached about the first of September, but the rate of decrease is not uniform. The solid residues, remaining after filtering, yield appreciable amounts of insoluble copper thruout the season. But, as with the soluble copper, the quantities showed marked fluctuations.

As regards arsenic, only very minute amounts become soluble but its appearance continues to the end. Most of the arsenic is recovered from the insoluble residues and it is interesting to note that the Bordeaux holds the Paris green tenaciously. Some particles were carried down by every rain that fell, even to the last on October 4, but in no case was the amount large.

TREE NUMBER 34

The equipment for tree No. 34 was similar to that provided for No. 33, but with this addition: a waterproof cover was supplied which was adjusted over the tree every evening and whenever there was immediate prospect of rain during the day, so that meteoric waters were effectually excluded. The tree was sprayed July 24 in a manner exactly like tree 33 and with a mixture made on the·same formula. When the spraying was completed the coating was as complete and the color of the leaves as blue as was tree 33. The funnel was then adjusted and the cover placed ready for use. The plan for this tree was, to substitute for natural rain, an artificial spray of cistern water applied at definite intervals of one week until four applications had been made. To this end an application was made July 31. The spray was directed upon the leaves thru a single Vermorel nozzle applied at a pressure of about 100 pounds from a barrel pump operated by hand, and in a manner to wash the leaves as thoroly as possible. The spraying continued for six minutes, and, after drip from the leaves had ceased, the water collected was removed, measured and sent to the chemical laboratory. The amount of the drip was 6.9 litres. Subsequent applications were made in like manner on August 7, 14 and 21. It would have been more satisfactory if uniform amounts of water had been applied, but this was neglected and the waters collected gradually increased. The second spray gave 8.96 litres, the third 9.06 litres, and the fourth 12.12 litres.

On completion of the spraying as previously planned, it was decided to dispense with the cover and collect the waters from rains thru the rest of the season, as with tree No. 33. Following this plan the waters of eleven rains were collected between August 24 and October 4. The analytical results for both spray waters and rain waters are brought together in the following tabulation:

Chemical Determinations of Waters Collected from Tree Number 34.

| Serial Number | Date | Amount of drip | Soluble constituents of drip waters | | | | | Sediment filtered from drip waters | | | |
| | | | Copper | | Alkalinity in terms of calcium oxide | | Arsenic in terms of As₂O₃ | Insoluble copper | | Insoluble arsenic | |
			Total Milligrams	Milligrams Per litre	Total Milligrams	Milligrams Per litre		Total Milligrams	Milligrams Per litre	Total Milligrams	Milligrams Per litre
34	July 31	6.39	412.0	64.4	36.0	5.6	1.1	971.6	152.0	143.5	22.4
34 a	August 7	8.96	241.6	26.9	30.0	3.3	3.6	896.8	100.8	61.2	6.8
34 b	August 14	9.06	81.2	8.9	26.3	2.9	2.3	398.4	43.9	88.2	9.7
34 c	August 21	12.12	90.0	7.4	16.3·	1.3	Trace	106.8	8.8	21.4	1.7
34 d	August 24	1.50	38.8	25.8	1.3	0.8	Trace	78.4	52.2	18.2	12.1
34 e	August 26	14.96	360.4	24.0	20.0	1.3	4.7	246.4	16.4	54.6	3.6
34 f	Sept. 3	1.25	26.0	20.8	Too dark	...	Trace	142.0	113.6	23.5	18.8
34 g	Sept. 13	1.53	56.4	36.8	Too dark	...	Trace	50.4	32.9	88.8	58.4
34 h	Sept. 20	1.70	50.4	29.6	0.20	...	Trace	282.8	166.3	66.5	39.3
34 i	Sept. 22	9.10	177.6	19.5	Neutral	...	Trace	182.4	20.0	35.5	5.0
34 j	Sept. 26	0.75	28.4	37.8	Neutral	...	Trace	84.0	112.0	40.6	54.1
34 k	Sept. 27	5.10	49.2	9.6	Neutral	...	Trace	100.8	19.7	45.5	8.9
34 l	Sept. 29	12.70	231.2	18.2	Neutral	...	3.5	84.0	6.6	46.2	3.6
34 m	October 1	14.82	194.0	13.0	Neutral	...	2.9	99.6	6.7	17.5	1.1
34 n	October 4	2.90	98.0	33.8	Too dark	...	2.4	56.0	19.3	Trace	....

Here again, soluble copper is found in the first drip waters collected, and in all succeeding waters. The amount of copper per litre decreases steadily for the four applications of water as spray, then with the first rain shows a considerable increase, which is maintained with some degree of uniformity to the end of the season. The alkalinity of the waters decreases steadily, reaching neutrality early in September. Arsenic in solution is present in very small quantities, mostly traces only in all waters. The quantities of insoluble copper and arsenic in the residues, fluctuate considerably, but both are present in all waters.

Injury to foliage on this tree was almost negligible. Casual examination revealed none, but on close inspection a few small marginal spots were found. These appeared after the cover had been discontinued and under the influence of the first rains, but were so few in number that they hardly deserve mention. Save for injury by the skeletonizer to some of the leaves expanded after application of the Bordeaux mixture, the foliage of the tree was very nearly perfect at the close of the season. As on tree 33, a few small leaves became yellow, and fell during the season. All remaining leaves were picked October 13 and preserved, for determination of copper still adhering.

TREE NUMBER 35

Sprayed July 25 in the same manner as trees 33 and 34 with a Bordeaux mixture made on the same formula. The funnel was then adjusted and cover provided to protect from rain and dew. One week from the application of Bordeaux, August 1, the tree was sprayed with cistern water and this was repeated at intervals of one week until the ninth application September 26. No further spraying was done and covering was discontinued. The tree was subjected to two rains October 4 and 20, and the drip waters were saved and analyzed. The chemical data obtained from the waters are given in tabular form below.

Chemical Determinations from Waters Collected from Tree Number 35.

Serial number	Date	Amount of drip	Soluble constituents of drip waters					Sediment filtered from drip waters			
			Copper		Alkalinity in terms of calcium oxide		Arsenic in terms of As_2O_3	Insoluble copper		Insoluble arsenic	
			Total Milligrams	Milligrams Per litre	Total Milligrams	Milligrams Per litre		Total Milligrams	Milligrams Per litre	Total Milligrams	Milligrams Per litre
5	August 1	9.47	79.6	8.4	141.8	14.9	6.3	1055.2	111.4	36.5	3.8
5 a	August 8	9.70	201.2	20.6	94.9	9.7	Trace	1174.0	121.0	49.2	5.0
5 b	August 15	12.94	320.8	24.7	67.3	5.2	Trace	870.8	67.2	45.5	3.5
5 c	August 22	11.43	67.6	5.9	127.7	11.1	Trace	527.2	46.1	38.3	3.3
5 d	August 29	11.48	174.0	15.1	4.7	0.4	Trace	321.6	28.0	35.0	3.0
5 e	Sept. 5	11.17	128.4	11.4	85.6	7.6	Trace	182.0	16.2	49.0	4.3
5 f	Sept. 12	11.50	656.8	57.1	5.8	0.5	Trace	89.6	7.7	46.2	4.0
5 g	Sept. 20	10.00	879.6	87.9	18.8	1.8	Trace	303.6	30.3	77.0	7.7
5 h	Sept. 26	10.65	652.8	61.2	40.9	3.8	Trace	46.8	4.4	13.3	1.2
5 i	Oct. 8	3.00	32.4	10.8	Too dark	Too dark	Trace	122.0	40.6	33.6	11.2
5 j	Oct. 20	15.90	903.2	56.7	Too dark	Too dark	10.6	53.6	3.3	20.3	1.2

Soluble copper was present in all waters from first to last. In the first lot, August 1, the amount is small, and still smaller in the fourth lot collected August 22. The last three sprays give considerably increased amounts, and the maximum appears in the lot of September 20. Alkalinity fluctuates, but is apparently more persistent than in the waters from preceding trees. Soluble arsenic was present in all waters, but except for the first and last, only as a trace. All residues from filtering yielded appreciable but fluctuating amounts of insoluble copper and arsenic.

Injury to foliage on tree 35 was as slight as on No. 34. Here it took the form of burned tips, but so few leaves were thus marked that the injury would easily escape notice.

TREE NUMBER 36

This tree duplicated Numbers 34 and 35 in equipment and cover, as well as in the manner and material of preliminary treatment. The spraying was done and the tree prepared July 28. Subsequent treatment was scheduled to include four applications of cistern water at seven day intervals; the fourth spray was to be followed by an interval of 28 days, and then a final spraying with water. This procedure was carried out in order to test the relation between time intervals and amount of soluble copper washed off by spray. The chemical results tabulated below, indicate that copper in soluble form did accumulate during the long interval:

Chemical Determinations from Waters Collected from Tree Number 36.

F Serial Number	Date	Amount of drip	Soluble constituents of drip waters					Sediment filtered from drip waters			
			Copper		Alkalinity in terms of calcium oxide		Arsenic in terms of As_2O_3	Insoluble copper		Insoluble arsenic	
			Total Milligrams	Milligrams Per litre	Total Milligrams	Milligrams Per litre		Total Milligrams	Milligrams Per litre	Total Milligrams	Milligrams Per litre
36	August 4	9.99	182.0	18.2	119.6	11.9	7.5	1214.4	121.5	90.6	9.0
36 a	August 11	11.11	237.6	21.3	148.0	13.3	3.7	309.6	27.8	30.6	2.7
36 b	August 18	10.55	130.0	12.3	35.6	3.3	1.3	211.2	20.0	32.9	3.1
36 c	August 25	9.68	117.6	12.1	42.4	4.3	1.1	160.0	16.4	31.8	3.2
36 d	Sept. 22	11.50	509.2	44.2	Too dark	....	7.9	726.0	63.1	159.2	13.8

The waters of the final spray applied at the end of a 28 day interval contained 44.2 milligrams of soluble copper per litre. This is more than twice the amount per litre shown from the first and second lots of water and more than 3½ times the quantities determined in the third and fourth lots, all these being taken at 7 day intervals. Computing the amounts of copper proportionate to the amounts of water collected, the application following the long interval still has more than twice as much copper as is found in the first and second, and over three times the amount in the third or fourth.

Arsenic in solution appears in descending scale for the four waters at 7 day intervals, and then increases, after the long interval, to an amount in excess of that found in the first water; the amount decreased with regularity to the fourth spraying and then, after the long interval, increased to nearly four times the amount in the water from the fourth spraying. Insoluble arsenic decreased in an irregular manner for the short periods, but in the last water, collected after the long interval, it was found in quantity greater than that of any two of the earlier lots.

FIG. 5. Tree No. 36. Cover adjusted, curtain down.

Foliage on this tree remained very nearly perfect. There were no brown spots, but search brought to view a few leaves that had slightly burned tips. When the leaves were finally gathered October 20 they were still conspicuously blue with Bordeaux mixture.

Tree No. 36 equipped with cover, and with curtain down, is shown in Figure 5. Figure 6 shows the same tree without cover and with curtain raised to show adjustment of jar. From photographs August 4, 1907.

SUMMARY OF RESULTS FROM THE FOUR TREES

The striking features of the records obtained from the four trees that have been considered are:

1. The constant presence of copper in solution. It was found in all waters examined, and except for the second rain on tree No. 33 from which the amount of water was too small for proper analysis, the quantities were measurable. It is true that the quantities are small,

FIG. 6. Tree No. 36. Cover removed. Curtain raised to show adjustment of
funnel to drip jar.

giving solutions that range between 1 part copper in 11,000 parts water and 1 part copper in 170,000 parts water; but it must be remembered that all the water collected did not come in contact with the leaves and that much that did made very hasty passage and probably took up very little copper, so that while solutions, as represented by the bulk of drip waters, are much diluted, it is reasonable to assume that on leaf surfaces, where the fungicidal action is wanted, the solutions are more concentrated and fully able to perform the office intended, namely, prevention of infection by germinating spores of fungi. The most dilute solution found, 1:170,000, is relatively quite concentrated if we compare it with a solution 2 or 3 to 10,000,000 which is stated by Millardet to be effective as a preventive of infection by *Peronospora*.

Fluctuations in the amount of copper in solution are to be expected and are influenced by many things, among which may be mentioned, direction of the storm, presence or absence of wind, velocity of wind, size of rain drops and duration of storm. The important point is that copper in soluble form is always present.

2. The appearance of soluble copper soon after the Bordeaux had been sprayed on the leaves. The mixtures used in the experiments recorded contained no copper in solution at the time of spraying. With each of the four trees the interval between application of Bordeaux and the first rain or spray of water was seven days. Soluble copper was found in these first waters collected under each of the four trees and in measurable quantities. Free calcium oxide was also present in quantity in these waters. This finding is directly contradictory to the statement by Millardet and Gayon and others that no copper becomes soluble until all free lime has been washed away or converted into insoluble carbonate. It is also opposed to the results obtained from the laboratory experiments already recorded, in which Bordeaux mixtures in glass dishes, both continuously dry and intermittently wet, yielded no soluble copper after 65 days, and in which two sprayed trees, one kept dry the other frequently moistened and after 45 days washed as thoroly as possible with neutral distilled water, gave no trace of copper in soluble form.

3. Examination of the results recorded, suggests another feature that is of sufficient importance to deserve specific mention, and that is the evidently slow solubility of the copper deposited in the Bordeaux mixture. The copper in solution fluctuates with different waters and at different times, but the amounts are always small, never in such excess as would indicate other than very slow solubility. Tree No. 33 was in commission for 84 days. The amount of copper per litre in the water from the last rain, 75 days from the date of spraying, was nearly double the amount in the first water collected 7 days after spraying. The waters of October 1 and 4 contained approximately the same as the waters of August 7 and 8. The maximum amount per litre appeared September 26, or 67 days from date of spraying. This slow solubility is one of the most valuable characteristics of rightly made Bordeaux. The copper becomes soluble with sufficient rapidity to maintain the defensive power, but not rapidly enough to dissipate quickly the reserve, and thus the action is prolonged for a long period.

4. A feature conspicuous in each of the four trees under consideration was the very great adhesiveness of the Bordeaux mixture. Notwithstanding the considerable quantity of water passed over the leaves, the blue color was remarkably persistent, particularly on the trees that were artificially sprayed. The tree without cover apparently

lost more of the Bordeaux than did those with covers, but even here the leaves were conspicuously coated when picked October 13, 84 days from the date of spraying. The tree was in some degree protected from wind by the funnel but otherwise the exposure was complete.

5. A fifth feature worthy of comment is the almost perfect condition of the leaves notwithstanding the extremely heavy application of Bordeaux. In no case was there sufficient injury to attract attention; such as was found by searching, consisted of small marginal burned spots and a few burned tips. Numerous heavily coated leaves remained without blemish until the close of the season.

Tree Number 49

This tree was provided with appliances for catching drip waters similar to those already described. The spraying was done August 23 in the same manner as for the other trees, but with a Bordeaux mixture combined with Arsenate of Lead instead of Paris green. The formula was as follows:

Copper sulphate.................................... 4 pounds
Fresh-slaked lime................................... 4 pounds
Swift's Arsenate of Lead.......................... 3 pounds
Water...50 gallons

About the time this work was instituted, the opinion was current among orchard owners that arsenate of lead could not be successfully combined with Bordeaux mixture. It was said that when combined the "one neutralized the other" and that both fungicidal and insecticidal value was destroyed. Who first disseminated this opinion or upon what observations it was based is not known. However, the frequency with which questions regarding the combination of these two compounds were asked made it desirable that definite information be secured through direct experiments. To this end tree Number 49 was sprayed with a combined mixture, made after the formula given above. Full exposure to dew and rain were allowed as with tree No. 33, but the two trees are not strictly comparable because tree No. 49 received a Bordeaux spray 33 days later than did No. 33 and was subjected to the waters of only about half the number of rains. When the mixture for use on tree No. 49 was prepared, two hydrometer tubes were filled, and the settling qualities tested. In this regard the arsenate of lead mixture exhibits a very slight advantage over the Paris green mixture for the first day, and a somewhat greater advantage at the end of the second day. The extreme of difference, however, is too small to be of importance from a practical standpoint. Between August 23 and October 4, the leaves of tree No. 49 were washed by the waters of 11 rains, giving precipitation to the amount of 3.3 inches, and the total of drip waters collected amounted to 65 litres. Soluble copper was present in all waters in measurable quantities. The amounts per litre fluctuate rather more widely than do the amounts in the waters from tree No. 33, but the averages are not widely separated, being 24.2 milligrams per litre for tree No. 49 and 29.18 milligrams per litre for tree No. 33. It is significant to note that the first rain came in less than 12 hours after spraying was completed; (a shower of 20 minutes duration giving rain fall of 0.06 inch and that the waters collected contain 2.8 milligrams of soluble copper per litre. This amount is small, but, coming as it does in less than 12 hours from deposition of a mixture containing no soluble copper, the result is interesting.

Arsenic in solution was detected in all waters, but in mere traces only. Insoluble arsenic was recovered from all waters and in considerably greater quantities than were shown to be present in corresponding waters from tree No. 33. On the other hand, insoluble copper was much more abundant in waters from tree No. 33 than from those from No. 49. Determinations made from the waters collected follow in tabular form:

Chemical Determinations from Waters Collected from Tree Number 49.

Serial number	Date	Amount of drip	Soluble constituents of drip waters					Sediment filtered from drip waters			
			Copper		Alkalinity in terms of calcium oxide		Arsenic in terms of As_2O_3	Insoluble copper		Insoluble arsenic	
			Total Milligrams	Milligrams Per litre	Total Milligrams	Milligrams Per litre		Total Milligrams	Milligrams Per litre	Total Milligrams	Milligram Per litre
9	August 24	1.64	4.6	2.8	45.1	27.5	Mere trace	36.1	22.0	Trace	....
9 a	August 27	13.92	74.4	5.3	154.8	11.1	" "	72.7	5.2	48.1	3.4
9 b	Sept. 3	1.25	104.4	83.5	Too dark	....	" "	38.2	30.5	24.7	19.7
9 c	Sept. 12	1.70	61.3	36.0	Too dark	....	" "	25.4	14.9	26.1	15.3
9 d	Sept. 20	1.80	9.8	5.4	Too dark	....	" "	28.7	15.9	22.5	12.5
9 e	Sept. 22	9.14	184.4	20.1	Too dark	....	" "	45.6	4.9	28.4	3.1
9 f	Sept. 26	.80	41.0	51.2	Too dark	....	" "	9.1	11.3	15.5	19.3
9 g	Sept. 27	5.45	53.4	9.8	Too dark	....	" "	64.3	11.7	30.9	5.6
9 h	Sept. 29	10.60	238.8	22.5	Neutral	....	" "	74.8	7.0	46.5	4.3
9 i	October 1	15.88	93.1	5.8	Neutral	....	" "	86.7	5.4	54.1	3.4
9 j	October 6	3.02	72.4	24.0	Too dark	....	" "	29.4	9.7	23.6	7.7

The behavior of the Bordeaux arsenate of lead combination as observed on this tree was very satisfactory. The mixture appears to possess exceptional adhesiveness and to part with its copper and arsenic at such a slow rate that its protective influence is prolonged to the end of the season. The proved presence of soluble copper, in all waters, indicated a continuous supply of this element in readiness for action against infection by fungi, and arsenic is retained in amounts sufficient to insure protection against insects. Nothing was observed during the season to indicate that any loss of fungicidal or insecticidal value followed the combination of the compounds in question. On the contrary continuous observation led to the belief that, so far as could be judged from the one experiment, the combination of Bordeaux with arsenate of lead has decided advantages over the Bordeaux Paris green mixture. The one valid objection is on the basis of cost, but it is expected that further trial may demonstrate that the additional expense is more than balanced by prolonged adhesiveness, efficiency, and entire absence of injury to foliage.

INVESTIGATIONS IN 1907

In 1906 spraying the trees from which drip waters were collected began July 21. This is rather late in the season, and the question arose as to whether applications applied earlier in the summer would show an equal degree of adhesiveness and as little injurious effect upon foliage. It was also desired to test somewhat further the relative influence of meteoric waters and artificially applied spray; to test the effect of maintaining an excess of calcium oxide by additional spraying with milk of lime and also several other questions suggested by the results already recorded.

For the season of 1907, therefore a considerably extended series of experiments was projected and carried out. Funnels and jars were provided, together with other necessary equipment, for 28 trees, which were used in pairs, for 14 experiments. Each experiment was given a number and the two trees were distinguished by the letters A and B. With two exceptions the trees of each pair were treated exactly alike. Under the Numbers 1107 A and B and 1207 A and B the individuals were differently treated, as will be explained later. The season proved to be a wet one; rains were frequent and abundant and the resources of the department were seriously taxed in handling the large amount of water. The experiments, however, were carried thru to the close of the season with very few minor accidents. A portion of the trees used for the experiments of 1907 are shown in Figure 7.

SCHEDULE OF EXPERIMENTS

No. 507—two trees—A and B. Sprayed heavily with standard Bordeaux-Paris green mixture. Exposed to all atmospheric conditions. To test the effect of meteoric waters on solubility of copper and the removal of excess lime. Duplicating No. 33 of the preceding year.

No. 607—two trees—A and B. Preliminary spray as for 507. Protection from meteoric waters. Sprayed with cistern water once each week. For comparison with 507 to test the relative effect of natural rain and water applied artificially as spray at regular intervals.

No. 707—two trees—A and B. Preliminary spray as for 507. Exposed to all atmospheric conditions. Sprayed with milk of lime 4–50 once each week. To test the influence of maintenance of excess lime on solubility of copper.

No. 807—two trees—A and B. No spray of Bordeaux. Exposed to all atmospheric conditions. Collect all drip from rains. Spray with milk of lime 4–50 once each week. To test the effect on foliage of milk of lime only. Compare with 707.

No. 907—two trees—A and B. Preliminary spray as for 507. Protection from meteoric waters, spray with cistern water once each week. Every Tuesday. Spray with milk of lime 4–50 each week. Every Friday. To test the effect of water as spray., in connection with milk of lime, in comparison with rain and milk of lime.

1007—two trees—A and B. Preliminary spray as for 507. Protection from meteoric waters. Spray once each week with water

FIG. 7. General view showing a portion of the trees used for the experiments of 1907. Photograph August 22, 1907.

saturated with carbon dioxide. To test the influence of carbon dioxide, in solution in water, on the solubility of copper.

1107—two trees A and B. Preliminary spray as for 507. Protection from meteoric waters. After an interval of several days.

A. Spray with 10 litres of cistern water, allow the tree to dry. Collect the water. Repeat as many times as possible during the day. To test the rate of removal of soluble copper under the action of continuous spraying. Repeat on a later date.

B. Spray with water to keep foliage moist all day with as little drip as possible. Remove drip at evening and then spray with about 10 litres of water and remove drip. Repeat on later date. To test long continuance of moist conditions.

1207—two trees, A and B. No spray of Bordeaux. Protection from meteoric waters.

A. Spray as for 1107 A, but use a solution of copper sulphate 50 mg to the gallon. In previous work, drip waters in several instances contained 50 mg or more per gallon. This is to test the action on foliage of such a solution artificially applied. The solution is quite dilute. 1:75707+.

B. Sprayed as for A but with a stronger solution 9.071 grams of copper sulphate to the gallon or 1:417+ To test the effect of a stronger solution and to determine the copper content of the drip.

1307—two trees—A and B. Preliminary spray as for 507. Protection from meteoric waters. Spray with distilled water once each week. To test distilled water as compared with cistern water in its effect on Bordeaux on leaves.

1407—two trees—A and B. Preliminary spray with standard formula Bordeaux made with air-slaked lime. Exposed to atmospheric conditions. To test action on foliage and adhesiveness of Bordeaux made with air-slaked lime.

1507—two trees—A and B. Preliminary spray with Bordeaux made on the formula 4–1–¼–50. Reducing the lime to 1 pound. Exposed to atmospheric conditions. To test effect on foliage of Bordeaux with reduced amount of lime.

1607—two trees—A and B. Preliminary spray with Bordeaux made after the formula 4–½–¼–50. Reducing the lime to ½ pound. Exposed to atmospheric conditions. To test this extreme reduction in the lime.

1707—two trees—A and B. Preliminary spray with Bordeaux mixture with lime reduced to 1 pound. 4–1–¼–50. Protection from meteoric waters. Spray once each week with water saturated with carbon dioxide. To test action of carbon dioxide, in solution in water, on Bordeaux made with small amount of lime.

1907—two trees—A and B. Preliminary spray with Bordeaux arsenate of lead combination, after the formula, 4–4–3–50, using Swift's paste arsenate of lead. Exposed to atmospheric conditions. To test the action on foliage, adhesiveness and rate of solubility of copper in this combination.

TREES 507 A AND 507 B COMPARED WITH NO. 33 OF 1906

The three trees, No. 33 of 1906, and Nos. 507 A and 507 B in 1907 were treated in exactly the same manner in regard to equipment, and preliminary spray. In length of time under observation, and in amount of rainfall to which the trees were subjected, there is a wide difference between the two seasons. In 1906, tree No. 33 was observed for 75 days; in 1907, trees 507 A and B were observed for 137 days or 1.82 times as many days. Tree No. 33 received 7.3 inches of rain from 21 storms, while the trees in 1907 received 13.36 inches from 24 storms. The amount of water collected in 1907 was nearly double the amount for 1906. The average number of litres in each lot of water was 6.2 for 1906, and 11.75 for 1907. All waters from tree No. 33 contained soluble copper altho in one lot there was only a trace.

From 507 A, there was one lot containing a trace only; from 507 B, one lot was lost thru accident. With these exceptions soluble copper was present in measurable amounts. The quantities, however, are much higher for 1906 than for either of the trees in 1907. The maxima in milligrams per litre are 85 for 1906, and 70 for 1907; the minima are 8.9 for 1906, and 0.7 for 1907. The averages are 23.5 milligrams per litre for 1906, and 9.2 for 1907, or stated proportionately there was 2½ times as much soluble copper per litre of water in 1906 as there was in 1907. It has already been mentioned that small quantities of water contained proportionately larger amounts of copper in solution per litre, than large quantities, and this fact is strongly emphasized in comparing the records under consideration.

Other seasonal differences that may be mentioned are intervals between rains, and character of storms. The longest intervals are nine days in 1906 and 21 days in 1907; the least intervals are 0 in 1906 and 12 hours in 1907; the averages are 3.16 days for 1906 and 5.6 days for 1907. Storms for the two seasons classify as follows:

	1906	1907
Local showers	11	6
Electrical storms	7	14
Protracted rains	3	4

It has been frequently suggested that there might be a definite relation between the character of the storm and the conversion of copper into soluble forms, with subsequent injury to foliage. Statements have been made to the effect that electrical phenomena often preceded the appearance of injury to foliage, and there has been an effort to connect the two. These things have been in mind during this investigation, and it may be said, that up to the present time, no evidence has been secured that points to electrical disturbances as in any way responsible for the passing of copper into solution and the following injury to foliage. The classification of storms, to which the trees used were subjected, shows that in 1907 there were twice as many electrical storms as in 1906, yet a decidedly larger amount of copper was found in 1906 than in 1907. The same wide difference in amounts of soluble copper, present in the waters from the trees of the two seasons, ap-

pears also in the determinations of insoluble copper found in the residues.   The average amount in the waters of 1906 is 246.7 milligrams,
with an average per litre of 54.3 milligrams, while from the waters of
1907 there was recovered an average of 155.5 milligrams with an average per litre of 20 milligrams.   It is evident that the copper of the
Bordeaux used in 1906 was more readily soluble and less tenaciously
held by the leaves than was the case in 1907 and it is probable that
more than one cause has operated to bring about this difference.
There may have been undiscovered differences in the mixtures as
made and applied.   While every precaution was taken in making and
in application, the lime in one case may have been a little less fresh, or

Chemical Determinations from Waters Collected from Tree 507 A.

Serial Number	Date	Amount of drip	Soluble constituents				Insoluble copper	
			Copper		Alkalinity in terms of calcium oxide			
			Total	Per litre	Total	Per litre	Total	Per litre
507 A 1	June 22	1.73	106.0	61.2	94.6	54.6	290.7	168.0
507 A 2	June 24	41.37	361.1	8.7	743.7	17.9	1186.2	28.6
507 A 3	July 1	2.44	14.1	5.7	86.7	35.5	216.1	88.5
507 A 4	July 6	9.58	Trace	....	290.6	30.3	414.5	43.2
507 A 5	July 9, 10	24.88	200.0	8.0	439.6	17.6	392.9	15.7
507 A 6	July 10, 11	9.79	84.5	8.6	154.4	15.7	117.8	12.0
507 A 7	July 14, 15	24.21	62.6	2.5	367.9	15.2	139.5	5.7
507 A 8	July 17	6.60	56.0	8.5	88.8	13.4	102.1	15.4
507 A 9	July 26	2.22	17.1	7.7	Too dark	....	14.7	6.6
507 A 10	July 28	6.71	60.5	9.0	47.7	7.1	23.6	3.5
507 A 11	July 31	16.73	183.8	10.9	144.6	8.6	84.5	5.0
507 A 12	August 1	.81	5.1	6.3	Too dark	....	Trace	....
507 A 13	August 5	21.22	254.8	12.0	57.3	2.7	53.0	2.4
507 A 14	August 7	17.52	117.0	6.6	325.2	18.5	25.5	1.4
507 A 15	August 12	4.82	88.2	18.3	36.7	7.6	25.5	5.3
507 A 16	August 16	28.79	105.7	3.6	236.2	8.1	110.0	3.8
507 A 17	August 17	4.65	3.2	0.7	95.4	20.5	47.1	10.1
507 A 18	August 20	8.26	56.9	6.8	90.7	10.9	21.6	2.6
507 A 19	Sept. 10	8.88	274.1	30.8	Too dark	....	106.1	11.9
507 A 20	Sept. 27	7.70	28.2	3.6	Too dark	....	265.2	34.4
507 A 21	October 3	18.00	9.0	0.5	Too dark	....	45.1	2.5
507 A 22	October 7	2.30	26.8	11.5	Too dark	....	5.9	2.5
507 A 23	October 15	2.40	10.0	4.1	Too dark	....	11.7	4.8
507 A 24	October 26	5.40	99.0	18.3	Too dark	....	23.6	4.3

sufficiently different in character from the other to render one mixture
more soluble and less adhesive than the other. Atmospheric conditions
other than amount of precipitation may have been responsible for the
recorded differences, but the necessary data for determination on this
point are not at hand.   For a period over 82 percent longer and a
precipitation of 45 percent greater in 1907 than in 1906 the natural
expectation would be the finding of a proportionately increased quantity of soluble copper in the waters collected in the later year.   The
results, however, are directly opposed to this expectation.   The quantity instead of being greater is considerably less.   Apparently time

period and amount of rain are not, in this case, the important factors in bringing copper into solution; that office rests in other less tangible factors that must be isolated, and proved thru more extended investigations.

The chemical data obtained from the drip waters from trees 507 A and 507 B appear in the tabulations pages 268 and 269.

Chemical Determinations from Waters Collected from Tree 507 B.

Serial Number	Date	Amount of Drip	Soluble constituents				Insoluble copper	
			Copper		Alkalinity in terms of calcium oxide			
			Total	Per litre	Total	Per litre	Total	Per litre
507 B 1	June 22	2.10	146.3	69.6	106.7	50.8	404.6	192.6
507 B 2	June 24	40.75	352.9	8.6	697.0	17.1	1125.6	27.6
507 B 3	July 1	2.50	28.2	11.2	94.8	37.9	27.5	11.0
507 B 4	July 6	9.49	79.9	8.4	238.1	25.0	392.9	41.4
507 B 5	July 9, 10	25.22	166.4	6.5	132.0	5.2	111.9	4.4
507 B 6	July 10, 11	9.82	40.9	4.1	150.9	15.3	35.3	3.5
507 B 7	July 14, 15	24.10	95.0	3.9	81.6	3.3	298.6	12.3
507 B 8	July 17	6.82	25.9	3.7	324.0	47.5	88.4	12.9
507 B 9	July 26	2.41	15.9	6.6	34.8	14.4	53.0	21.9
507 B 10	July 28	6.83	40.1	5.8	103.2	15.1	70.7	10.3
507 B 11	July 31	16.98	74.6	4.3	258.0	15.1	66.4	3.9
507 B 12	August 1	Lost	....	....	....	....	....	....
507 B 13	August 5	20.28	56.5	2.7	588.1	29.0	39.3	1.9
507 B 14	August 7	17.22	115.9	6.7	66.7	3.8	29.4	1.7
507 B 15	August 12	5.12	86.7	16.9	24.8	4.8	25.5	4.9
507 B 16	August 16	28.93	40.6	1.4	220.6	7.6	31.4	1.0
507 B 17	August 17	4.92	8.4	1.7	56.3	11.4	27.5	5.5
507 B 18	August 20	7.95	39.0	4.9	125.5	15.7	39.3	4.9
507 B 19	Sept. 10	9.11	66.4	7.2	273.3	30.0	45.2	4.9
507 B 20	Sept. 27	7.50	61.6	8.2	Too dark	....	58.9	7.8
507 B 21	October 3	17.60	27.1	1.5	Too dark	....	17.6	1.0
507 B 22	October 7	2.40	1.6	0.6	Too dark	....	9.7	4.0
507 B 23	October 15	2.42	6.6	2.7	Too dark	Neutr'l	8.4	3.5
507 B 24	October 26	5.03	29.4	5.8	Too dark	Neutr'l	7.8	1.5

The foliage of trees 507 A and 507 B was not injured to any serious extent and yet there were more leaves marked by brown spots and brown marginal areas than appeared on any of the five trees treated in 1906. The trees were sprayed June 11. No injury followed immediately after spraying, nor was any observed for several weeks. August 12 brown spots, few in number and small in size were observed on a few leaves; they did not come all at once, but appeared to develop a few at a time. In making daily observations, it was difficult to detect changes in appearance from day to day, but by September 4 the spots were numerous enough to attract attention. As the season advanced and the blue coating of Bordeaux became somewhat thin by repeated washing, the spots became still more conspicuous; this was largely the result of the distribution over the trees. A large majority of the leaves were uninjured and remained so to the close of the season, but the few that were injured were so mingled with the perfect leaves as to give the impression of a greater amount of injury than really existed. Why two or three leaves among the 15 or 20 on a twig should be injured, while all others remain intact, is usually not answerable from direct or even from critical examination. The brown spots are not seen to develop; an examination one day shows all leaves perfect; on next examination spots are there. Possible causes can be suggested, but the essential proof of action of any suggested cause, is in most cases, wanting. Some suggested causes may be disposed of by processes of elimination; these are the least complex; thus, the larger quantity of mixture deposited on leaves is eliminated as a cause of injury by the frequent observation that leaves carrying very small amounts are fully as liable to injury as are the more heavily coated. In like manner the matters of location, size of leaf, and certain atmospheric conditions can be dismissed by observation, as inoperative factors. This narrows the investigation to those less tangible, more obscure factors that involve nutritive and other organic functions of living plants. In some cases degree of injury appears to be influenced by the health and vigor of growth of the plants. This is illustrated by the trees here considered. Number 507 A made a much stronger growth during the season than did No. 507 B; its general appearance indicated a degree of vitality not shown by B. The number of injured leaves and the extent of injury on individuals was noticeably greater on 507 B than on 507 A. The brown spots noted on these two trees appeared between August 12 and September 4; from this last date on thru September and October, no increase in number or size of spots could be detected. Why development of injury was confined to the period named has not been determined. But it cannot be ascribed to any excess of soluble copper present at that particular time. The average amounts of soluble copper during the period from June 11, the date of spraying, to the appearance of injury, and again for the period from September 4 to the close of the season were both greater than during the time of development of injury.

Yellow leaves. During the long interval between rains, August 20 to September 10, a few leaves became yellow. Twelve of the sprayed leaves were thus affected, but as a somewhat greater number of leaves on new shoots above, that had not been sprayed, became yellow, at the same time, yellowing can not have been caused by any direct action of the spray. These yellow leaves were all carried down by the rain of September 10 and there was no further appearance of yellowing. When the leaves were picked from the trees October 31, it was noted that every leaf that had been sprayed carried evident traces of Bordeaux, and many were still well covered.

COMPARISON OF TREES SUBJECTED TO RAIN, WITH TREES SPRAYED WITH CISTERN WATER

The trees exposed to rains were the trees that have been already treated, namely, 507 A and B. These were sprayed with the Bordeaux-Paris green mixture June 11 and subjected to 24 rains, giving precipitation of 13.36 inches during the period of 137 days ending with the last rain October 26. With these may be compared two adjacent trees—numbers 607 A and 607 B—which were sprayed in exactly the same manner on the same day. Covers were provided to protect from rain and dew, and the two trees were sprayed at seven-day intervals, with cistern water, in amounts varying from 6½ to 11 litres. There were 18 applications in all between June 18 and October 15. The period between preliminary spray and the last spray of rain water is 126 days. The waters collected from the trees subjected to rain were 76.069 percent greater in quantity than those from the trees sprayed with water, and they contained 2.38 times as much soluble copper. The average amount of copper is 9.06 milligrams per litre for the 507 trees, and 5.17 milligrams per litre for the 607 trees. Soluble copper was present in all waters from rains, and ranged in amount between a trace in the fourth water from tree 507 A, to 70 milligrams per litre in the first water from 507 B. Of the trees sprayed with cistern water, No. 607 A yielded small amounts of soluble copper to every lot of drip collected. The quantities varied from 0.6 milligrams per litre in the water of October 1 to 11.1 milligrams per litre in the water of September 3. No. 607 B yielded soluble copper to 17 of the 18 lots of water, in amounts between 0.5 milligram per litre and 15.9 milligrams per litre. The seventh water, from the spray of July 30 gave no trace of soluble copper. In general, the amounts of copper in the spray waters, applied at regular intervals in fairly uniform quantities, show much less fluctuation than do the amounts from rains which were widely variable in amount and at very irregular intervals. The amount of soluble copper per litre is much greater in the waters from rains than in the spray waters. This is probably the result of several active causes; the much greater quantity of water that passed over the leaves; the carbon dioxide and ammonia carried by meteoric waters; heavy dews; the greater mechanical action of falling rain drops; and, in general, the more complete exposure to atmospheric conditions.

The most striking contrast between the two pairs of trees, is the entire absence of brown spotting and yellowing of leaves on the trees sprayed with water. There is also a certain advantage in size of leaves, an appearance of health and sound vitality and an unusually dark green color that is all on the side of the foliage protected from rain and sprayed with cistern water. The foliage on the 507 trees is good, and, as compared with unsprayed leaves, shows considerably darker shades of green, but depth of color is more pronounced in the leaves of the 607 trees, and this, in connection with the absolutely perfect condition, gives the water sprayed trees a decided advantage when compared with the trees exposed to rain. In the matter of the adhesiveness of Bordeaux, the advantage is also with the 607 trees. This is in great part accounted for by the fact that spray delivered as a fine mist, has much less mechanical action in loosening and removing the coating of Bordeaux than heavier rain drops, especially when the latter are driven by wind. The 607 trees were almost as intensely blue at the time of the last spraying, October 15, as on the day of application, June 11, while the blue of the 507 trees was considerably diminished.

Summarizing all the observations made upon the trees under consideration, it is concluded that meteoric waters have the power of converting the copper of Bordeaux mixture into soluble forms at a more rapid rate than have waters applied as spray. This is probably due to the carbon dioxide and ammonia contained in rains, but may in part be ascribed to differences in mechanical action, to heavy dews and more complete exposure to the action of the atmosphere.

Chemical Determinations from Waters Collected from Trees 607 A and 607 B.

Serial Number	Date		Amount litres	Soluble constituents.			
				Copper		Alkalinity in terms of calcium oxide	
				Total	Per litre	Total	Per litre
607 A 1	June	18	9.56	30.4	3.1	200.2	20.9
607 A 2	June	25	8.00	55.3	6.9	437.9	54.7
607 A 3	July	2	8.92	43.6	4.8	263.7	29.5
607 A 4	July	9	9.91	78.9	7.9	272.0	27.4
607 A 5	July	16	7.58	46.2	6.0	151.0	19.9
607 A 6	July	23	8.43	12.9	1.5	126.8	15.0
607 A 7	July	30	6.51	29.9	4.5	118.9	18.2
607 A 8	August	6	10.36	46.3	4.4	184.0	17.7
607 A 9	August	13	8.72	53.0	6.0	130.8	15.0
607 A 10	August	20	7.43	8.6	1.1	235.5	31.6
607 A 11	August	27	9.23	12.7	1.3	329.5	35.6
607 A 12	Sept.	3	7.88	88.0	11.1	187.7	23.8
607 A 13	Sept.	10	8.73	49.5	5.6	641.1	73.4
607 A 14	Sept.	17	9.62	44.4	4.6	164.0	17.0
607 A 15	Sept.	24	8.73	21.2	2.4	169.1	19.3
607 A 16	October	1	8.17	5.1	0.6	133.9	16.3
607 A 17	October	8	9.60	27.5	2.8	307.3	32.0
607 A 18	October	15	11.00	45.1	4.1	221.6	20.1
607 B 1	June	18	8.56	5.1	0.59	105.2	12.2
607 B 2	June	25	9.08	46.8	5.1	419.2	46.1
607 B 3	July	2	7.42	27.3	3.6	234.6	31.6
607 B 4	July	9	8.33	126.7	15.2	272.0	32.6
607 B 5	July	16	8.33	41.3	4.9	185.6	22.2
607 B 6	July	23	7.18	17.7	2.4	150.2	20.9
607 B 7	July	30	7.53	None	....	96.2	12.7
607 B 8	August	6	7.61	32.2	4.2	115.8	15.2
607 B 9	August	13	9.61	44.7	4.6	146.7	15.2
607 B 10	August	20	8.09	32.8	4.0	146.0	18.0
607 B 11	August	27	7.60	28.3	3.7	274.7	36.1
607 B 12	Sept.	3	7.50	45.9	6.1	180.5	24.0
607 B 13	Sept.	10	8.37	133.1	15.9	777.2	92.8
607 B 14	Sept.	17	10.45	5.9	0.5	343.3	32.8
607 B 15	Sept.	24	9.07	87.6	9.6	87.1	9.6
607 B 16	October	1	9.13	134.3	14.7	86.4	9.4
607 B 17	October	8	8.25	71.6	8.6	281.3	34.0
607 B 18	October	15	7.62	21.1	2.7	103.0	13.5

The entire absence of injury to foliage, of the 607 trees, may be in some measure accounted for in the less amount of soluble copper shown to be present in the waters, but it is thought that at times the copper in solution was present in sufficient amount to be injurious, had other conditions been favorable. The foliage of the trees exposed to rain is kept moist for a much longer period at the time of each rain, than is the case with the sprayed trees. In spraying, the application requires from 5 to 7 minutes and within an hour the foliage is dry again, while the trees exposed to rain have the leaves continuously wet for periods ranging from two or three hours to more than twenty-four hours.

Various experiments indicate that long continued moisture is, in many cases a controlling factor in causing injury to foliage. But it is not operative in all cases; hence there must be other contributory causes, such as condition of the atmosphere, character of the rain, matters in solution in the rain water, temperature, and the state of vitality of the leaves. To isolate all possible agencies that may contribute to injurious action, test by experiment and prove the connection of each in such manner as will allow unconditional conclusions will require much more extended investigations than have yet been made in this direction. The chemical data obtained from trees 607 A and 607 B, so far as completed, are given in tabular form page 272.

MAINTAINING AN EXCESS OF LIME

For the purpose of testing the effects of continuously maintained excess of lime upon foliage and upon the solubility of the copper deposited in Bordeaux mixture, six trees, in three pairs, were used. The trees were given the numbers 707 A and B, 807 A and B and 907 A and B. Each tree was equipped with funnel, jar and other accessories necessary for catching the drip, just as described for other trees. Each test is made in duplicate because the average of results from two trees is better basis for conclusions than results from a single tree; one serves as a check upon the other. If wide fluctuations occur between the results from two trees that receive exactly the same treatment, something is probably wrong with one or the other; and the cause of the difference must be traced out and explained. In the experiments to be described there was remarkable uniformity in the results from the two trees of each pair.

June 11 the 707 pair and the 907 pair were heavily sprayed with the Bordeaux-Paris green mixture made after the usual 4–4–¼–50 formula. Covers were provided for the 907 pair to protect the trees from all rain and dew, while the 707 pair was left exposed to rains. Tree No. 907 A with its equipment is shown in Figure 8.

Commencing June 18, seven days after the application of Bordeaux, the 707 trees were sprayed with milk of lime, 4 pounds to 50 gallons, and this was repeated at intervals of one week until October 15, making a total of 18 applications, in amounts averaging about 8 litres. Between June 22, the date of first rain, and October 26, the date of last rain, the trees were washed by the waters of 24 rains giving a precipitation of 13.36 inches. Adding the rains and sprays we have a total of 42 lots of water collected from each of the two trees. The gross amount of water collected was a little more than 376 litres per tree, or an average of nearly 9 litres for each lot. The 907 trees, those protected from rain, were sprayed with cistern water June 18

one week after the application of Bordeaux.   This was repeated at intervals of one week until October 15, thus giving 18 applications, in
amounts averaging about 8 litres. June 21 the same trees were sprayed
with milk of lime (4–50) and this was repeated at weekly intervals
until the number of applications equalled the number given of cistern
water.   This brought the last spray October 18.   The amounts at each
application averaged about the same as for the cistern water.   From

Fig. 8. Tree 907A, covered. Curtain raised to show drip jar.
From photograph October 17, 1907.

each of these trees, therefore, 36 lots of water were collected.   The
gross amount of water was a fraction less than 300 litres per tree,
with an average of $8\frac{1}{3}$ litres per lot.

The 807 pair of trees was used solely to test the action upon foliage of a continuously maintained excess of lime in connection with
free exposure to rain.   The trees were sprayed with the same milk of
lime, on the same dates, and in approximately the same amounts as

were applied on the 707 trees. The only difference between the two pairs is that the 807 pair received no preliminary spray. No Bordeaux was at any time used on these trees. The number of waters collected, 24 from rains and 18 from sprays, is the same as collected from the 707 trees, and the gross amount of water per tree is approximately the same.

INFLUENCE OF LIME IN EXCESS ON THE SOLUBILITY OF COPPER

Comparing the 707 trees with the 907 trees in the matter of copper in solution, the most striking feature is the irregularity in the appearance of soluble copper in the waters from all four trees. Of the 42 waters collected from the 707 trees, 26 from 707 A and 29 from 707 B contain soluble copper; hence 16 from A and 13 from B were free from copper. Of the 16 lots from 707 A that contain no copper, 12 were from milk of lime sprays and 4 were from rains. Separating the corresponding copper free lots from 707 B, gives 8 from lime sprays and five from rains.

In these waters containing copper, the amounts are, in general, quite small. The maximum for 707 A is 56 milligrams per litre, for 707 B—33.3 milligrams per litre, both from the second water collected from a rain of 0.1 inch on June 22. The minimum is a fraction of a milligram for both trees. Turning to the covered trees it is seen that of the 36 lots of water, 13 from 907 A and 14 from 907 B contain copper; this leaves 23 lots from A and 22 lots from B that were free from copper. Separating these copper free lots, according to the kind of spray, shows that 15 of the A lots and 12 of the B lots were lime sprays, while 8 of the A lots and 10 of the B lots were from sprays of cistern water. The maximum of copper in milligrams per litre, is 6.3 in the first water from A and 4.0 in the third water from B.

The difference between the two pairs of trees in amounts of soluble copper, is perhaps best shown in the averages of milligrams per litre, computed from the waters containing copper; these are, for the 707 pair 4.2 milligrams per litre and for the 907 pair 1.7 milligrams per litre. The averages in both are low, but the trees exposed to rains show nearly 2½ times as much as the trees protected and receiving water by spray only.

Combining the figures from the two trees of each pair and stating the copper differences in percentages, it is found that 65.47 percent of the 707 and only 37.5 percent of the 907 waters contain soluble copper. Of the waters containing no copper 69 percent of the 707, and 60 percent of the 907 waters were collected from lime sprays. That the superabundance of lime does act in an effective manner to check the conversion of copper into soluble forms is evident from the figures given. It is also evident that its influence is most potent where meteoric waters are excluded. Comparing the trees sprayed with lime with the 507 and 607 pairs previously discussed it may be noted that waters from the 507 pair, which was subjected to meteoric waters only, contained 2.15 times the number of milligrams of soluble copper per litre as did the waters from the 707 pair which was washed by the same rains, but was also given 18 applications of milk of lime. Also that waters from the 607 pair sprayed 18 times with cistern water, yielded 3.04 times as many milligrams of soluble copper per litre as was found in the waters of the 907 pair treated in exactly the same

Chemical Determinations from Waters Collected from Tree 707 A.

Serial Number	Date	Amount of drip	Soluble Constituents			
			Copper		Alkalinity in terms of calcium oxide	
			Total	Per litre	Total	Per litre
707 A 1	June 18	6.20	None	....	7118.2	1148.1
707 A 2	June 22	1.73	97.0	56.0	72.4	41.8
707 A 3	June 24	36.64	44.8	1.2	1402.3	38.2
707 A 4	June 25	4.19	None	....	3088.0	736.9
707 A 5	July 1	2.41	12.5	5.1	222.4	92.2
707 A 6	July 2	5.30	None	....	5330.8	1005.8
707 A 7	July 6	10.22	66.8	6.5	618.3	60.5
707 A 8	July 9	8.01	None	....	7976.6	995.7
707 A 9	July 9, 10	24.76	17.8	0.7	1452.1	58.6
707 A 10	July 10, 11	9.84	None	....	431.1	43.8
707 A 11	July 14, 15	23.42	121.0	5.1	1223.7	52.3
707 A 12	July 16	5.55	15.7	2.8	4376.6	788.5
707 A 13	July 17	7.60	39.2	5.1	603.7	79.4
707 A 14	July 23	6.76	93.8	13.9	7505.5	1110.2
707 A 15	July 26	1.96	21.0	10.7	47.8	24.3
707 A 16	July 28	6.70	7.4	1.1	252.6	37.7
707 A 17	July 30	8.15	None	....	7851.0	963.3
707 A 18	July 31	16.31	78.5	4.8	454.8	27.8
707 A 19	August 1	.72	Trace	Trace	72.7	100.9
707 A 20	August 5	21.17	30.5	1.4	2430.1	114.7
707 A 21	August 6	7.22	None	....	9201.3	1274.3
707 A 22	August 7	17.83	16.5	0.9	2187.8	122.7
707 A 23	August 12	4.66	None	....	257.0	55.1
707 A 24	August 13	6.63	None	....	7169.6	1081.3
707 A 25	August 16	28.59	29.4	1.0	1924.3	673.0
707 A 26	August 17	4.12	19.0	4.6	323.4	78.2
707 A 27	August 19	8.15	28.5	3.4	377.1	46.2
707 A 28	August 20	5.08	23.3	4.5	6320.0	1240.0
707 A 29	August 27	5.40	1.5	0.2	7065.9	1308.8
707 A 30	Sept. 3	3.89	11.8	3.0	4752.4	1221.7
707 A 31	Sept. 9, 10	5.99	8.6	1.4	Too dark	....
707 A 32	Sept. 10	6.93	None	....	7861.5	1134.4
707 A 33	Sept. 17	5.19	None	....	6452.9	1243.3
707 A 34	Sept. 24	9.13	9.0	9.8	10598.8	1160.7
707 A 35	Sept. 26, 27	7.50	None	....	Too dark	......
707 A 36	October 1	6.50	None	....	8335.1	1282.3
707 A 37	October 3	16.41	None	....	785.1	47.8
707 A 38	October 7	2.00	7.0	3.5	65.9	32.9
707 A 39	October 8	7.10	None	....	7903.3	1113.1
707 A 40	October 15	2.07	6.6	3.1	364.1	175.8
707 A 41	October 15	6.57	None	....	6667.9	1014.9
707 A 42	October 28	5.18	9.7	1.8	Too dark	......

manner except for the weekly applications of milk of lime. The results of this test give additional proof of the greater effectiveness of meteoric waters as compared with artificial spray, in converting the copper of Bordeaux mixture into soluble form. They also show that while lime in great excess diminished the amount, it did not entirely prevent formation of soluble copper.

Soluble copper and free lime, as determined for the waters from the trees last considered, are given in tabular form on pages 276–277 and 279–280. Insoluble constituents have not yet been determined.

Chemical Determinations from Waters Collected from Tree 707 B.

Serial Number	Date	Amount of drip	Soluble constituents			
			Copper		Alkalinity in terms of calcium oxide	
			Total	Per litre	Total	Per litre
707 B 1	June 18	6.17	None	....	7254.3	1175.6
707 B 2	June 22	2.09	68.0	32.5	78.9	37.7
707 B 3	June 24	35.71	162.5	4.5·	1378.6	38.6
707 B 4	June 27	6.86	5.2	0.7	6516.1	949.8
707 B 5	July 1	2.38	8.6	3.6	60.2	2.52
707 B 6	July 2	7.46	9.4	1.2	5495.5	736.6
707 B 7	July 6	8.87	36.6	4.1	325.0	36.6
707 B 8	July 9	6.97	16.4	2.3	6280.0	901.0
707 B 9	July 9, 10	24.68	10.3	0.4	884.5	35.8
707 B 10	July 10, 11	10.39	27.5	2.6	472.1	45.4
707 B 11	July 14, 15	22.40	15.0	0.6	623.9	27.8
707 B 12	July 16	6.52	3.2	0.4	6353.6	974.4
707 B 13	July 17	7.15	12.0	1.6	536.7	75.0
707 B 14	July 23	7.26	4.8	0.6	7998.6	1101.7
707 B 15	July 26	2.27	3.4	1.4	87.4	38.5
707 B 16	July 28	6.47	6.6	1.0	161.6	24.9
707 B 17	July 30	7.22	5.9	0.8	6943.1	961.6
707 B 18	July 31	16.32	37.7	2.3	429.2	26.3
707 B 19	August 1	.93	None	....	41.7	44.8
707 B 20	August 5	19.68	11.8	0.6	581.4	29.5
707 B 21	August 6	5.78	None	....	7222.9	1249.4
707 B 22	August 7	16.34	10.4	0.6	879.3	53.8
707 B 23	August 12	4.88	23.3	4.7	273.4	56.0
707 B 24	August 13	6.07	None	....	6451.7	1062.8
707 B 25	August 16	28.16	37.7	1.3	1104.3	39.2
707 B 26	August 17	4.55	None	....	296.7	65.2
707 B 27	August 19	7.79	10.6	1.3	465.8	59.7
707 B 28	August 20	5.14	None	....	6270.8	1220.0
707 B 29	August 27	5.45	2.5	0.4	6908.8	1267.5
707 B 30	Sept. 3	5.38	2.6	0.4	6437.8	1196.4
707 B 31	Sept. 9, 10	5.63	3.4	0.6	Too dark	......
707 B 32	Sept. 10	8.19	None	....	5992.9	731.7
707 B 33	Sept. 17	6.20	3.1	0.5	3044.2	491.0
707 B 34	Sept. 24	6.20	None	....	7222.9	1165.0
707 B 35	Sept. 26, 27	6.94	None	....	497.2	71.6
707 B 36	October 1	6.20	6.1	0.9	7693.9	1240.9
707 B 37	October 3	15.55	9.8	0.6	821.7	52.8
707 B 38	October 7	2.10	2.3	1.0	71.0	33.8
707 B 39	October 8	3.55	None	....	4671.6	1315.9
707 B 40	October 15	3.10	None	....	Too dark	......
707 B 41	October 15	7.76	None	....	8216.4	1058.8
707 B 42	October 26	4.71	None	....	Too dark	......

CONDITION OF FOLIAGE OF TREES SPRAYED WITH LIME

Foliage of the 707 trees was in excellent condition thruout the season. The first spray of milk of lime obscured the blue color of the Bordeaux and gave a white coating which was still retained when the leaves were picked October 31. Both trees made a vigorous growth, the new shoots finally overtopping the funnel by two feet or more. About the middle of July the large size of the individual leaves of these trees attracted attention and comparisons were made with leaves from adjacent trees of the same variety that had not been sprayed. The sprayed leaves were evidently larger. This observation was repeated several times at intervals during the following months and the comparison was extended to include all the trees sprayed with lime, the 507 trees sprayed with Bordeaux only, as well as trees that had not been sprayed. The six trees receiving applications of lime shared the advantage in the matter of size. From all of them the leaves averaged distinctly larger than leaves from the other trees. No difference could be detected between leaves from the trees sprayed with Bordeaux mixture and milk of lime, and those sprayed only with milk of lime. The aggregate of observations suggests a stimulating action on the part of the lime, that had operated in the direction of increase in size; whether by direct action upon the leaves, or by reason of the protective covering afforded, is not apparent. It is hoped that further investigation of the action here involved can be undertaken during the present season.

Observations and comparisons were also made at frequent intervals upon the color of leaves. These gave very uniform results which lead to the conclusion that Bordeaux mixture has a decided influence upon color. Under a coating of Bordeaux the leaf becomes much deeper green and this darker color is retained even after the coating is mostly washed away. Contrasted with leaves of equal age and similar location that had not been sprayed with Bordeaux the difference is very striking. Leaves coated with lime only become somewhat darker than leaves not treated, but the shade of green is not so deep as is assumed under a coating of Bordeaux.

No burning or other injury to foliage was observed on the 707 trees until September 4; on that date, a few brown marginal spots were discovered on some of the lower leaves. The number of these spots did not appear to increase, and individual spots remained small, as when first discovered. Notes taken October 19th say—"Very few brown spots. A few of the lower leaves have each from 1 to 3 small brown marginal areas, but the injury is insignificant."

The 807 trees sprayed with milk of lime only, remained entirely free from brown spots or burned margins thruout the season. The experience with these trees shows that lime alone has little adhesiveness; the trees are white immediately after spraying, but the coating scales off quite readily and each rain removed nearly all that remained. Comparison with the 707 trees, indicates that the Bordeaux acts as a binder, that holds the lime upon the leaves for some time. The 907 trees protected .from rain and sprayed alternately with lime and cistern water, retained the leaves in perfect condition to the end of the season.

Yellow leaves: During the examination of the 707 trees on September 4, it was observed that a few leaves scattered over the trees

Chemical Determinations from Waters Collected from Tree 907 A.

Serial Number	Date		Amount of drip	Soluble constituents			
				Copper		Alkalinity in terms of calcium oxide	
				Total	Per litre	Total	Per litre
907 A 1	June	18	6.10	38.8	6.3	202.6	33.2
907 A 2	June	21	3.64	6.6	1.8	4187.2	1150.3
907 A 3	June	25	10.90	43.2	3.9	447.5	41.0
907 A 4	June	28	5.91	None	....	5835.9	987.4
907 A 5	July	5	7.56	9.4	1.2	549.6	72.7
907 A 6	July	5	7.68	None	....	7144.4	930.2
907 A 7	July	9	10.93	4.7	0.4 ·	293.1	26.8
907 A 8	July	12	5.71	None	....	6620.0	1159.4
907 A 9	July	16	9.81	46.4	4.7	274.6	28.0
907 A 10	July	19	8.92	None	....	7981.8	894.8
907 A 11	July	23	7.19	11.7	1.6	361.7	50.3
907 A 12	July	26	6.97	10.3	1.3	7181.0	1030.2
907 A 13	July	30	5.46	None	....	250.4	45.8
907 A 14	August	2	6.19	None	....	6673.3	1078.0
907 A 15	August	6	10.65	None	....	497.8	46.7
907 A 16	· August	9	8.39	None	....	10041.4	1196.7
907 A 17·	August	13	7.95	None	....	272.1	34.2
907 A 18	August	16	8.38	None	....	10598.8	1264.7
907 A 19	August	20	8.70	8.6	0.9	674.4	77.5
907 A 20	August	23	9.29	None	....	11786.9	1268.7
907 A 21	August	27	9.70	None	....	669.4	69.0
907 A 22	August	30	9.33	13.6	1.4	11549.3	1237.8
907 A 23	Sept.	3	11.48	5.4	0.4	523.4	45.5
907 A 24	Sept.	6	6.75	None	....	8565.4	1268.8
907 A 25	Sept.	10	8.70	1.9	0.2	455.3	52.3
907 A 26	Sept.	13	7.90	None	.... ·	9709.0	1229.0
907 A 27	Sept.	17	9.01	None	....	376.8	41.8
907 A 28	Sept.·	20	7.11	None	....	9342.7	1313.9
907 A 29	Sept.	24	11.27	9.7	0.8	259.1	22.9
907 A 30	Sept.	27	8.30	None	....	10446.1	1258.5
907 A 31	October	1	7.77	None	....	212.7	27.4
907 A 32	October	4	9.09	None	....	10337.1	1137.1
907 A 33	October	8	8.27	None	....	223.0	26.9
907 A 34	October	11	8.05	None	·	9106.1	1131.1
907 A 35	October	15	7.40	None	....	314.0	42.4
907 A 36	October 18		10.04	None	....	11136.0	1109.1

were in part yellow or had assumed the light greenish yellow color that precedes complete yellowing. These leaves became entirely yellow and fell with the rain the evening of September 9. There were 14 from 707 A and 20 from 707 B. At this same time, leaves in about the same numbers became yellow and fell from the 807 trees. Similar yellowing occurred on the 507 trees, as has already been mentioned. The yellowing on the 807 trees, which received no Bordeaux, occurring coincident with that on the other trees referred to, and also on many trees that had not been sprayed, indicated some cause other than Bordeaux. A sufficient number of trees were affected with yellowing concurrently, to give the appearance of an epidemic, altho a very mild one. The cause is not known, but may lie in some atmospheric or soil condition. It is significant that the 907 trees did not, at this, or any other time during the season, show a single yellow leaf.

Chemical Determinations from Waters Collected from Tree 907 B.

Serial number	Date		Amount of drip	Soluble constituents			
				Copper		Alkalinity in terms of calcium oxide	
				Total	Per litre	Total	Per litre
907 B 1	June	18	7.69	None	....	214.7	27.9
907 B 2	June	21	4.62	11.7	2.5	5443.3	1178.2
907 B 3	June	25	10.42	42.6	4.0	471.5	45.2
907 B 4	June	28	7.76	None	....	7461.7	957.8
907 B 5	July	2	10.22	30.2	2.9	783.4	76.6
907 B 6	July	5	9.68	3.2	0.3	9185.6	948.9
907 B 7	July	9	9.51	4.2	0.4	276.4	29.0
907 B 8	July	12	9.94	None	....	8923.9	897.7
907 B 9	July	16	10.90	15.7	1.4	494.6	45.3
907 B 10	July	19	7.03	9.8	1.3	7327.6	1042.3
907 B 11	July	23	8.22	None	....	357.3	43.4
907 B 12	July	26	9.94	8.0	0.8	10596.2	1066.0
907 B 13	July	30	8.77	23.2	2.6	794.1	90.5
907 B 14	August	2	9.75	None	....	10331.9	1059.6
907 B 15	August	6	10.11	None	....	481.7	47.6
907 B 16	August	9	8.88	None	....	10468.0	1178.8
907 B 17	August	13	7.69	None	....	186.7	24.2
907 B 18	August	16	9.15	None	....	11373.5	1243.0
907 B 19	August	20	9.50	6.1	0.6	720.9	75.8
907 B 20	August	23	6.96	2.9	0.4	9002.5	1293:5
907 B 21	August	27	7.53	3.1	0.4	548.1	72.7
907 B 22	August	30	6.10	4.2	0.7	7502.9	1229.8
907 B 23	Sept.	3	6.75	10.8	1.6	405.6	60.0
907 B 24	Sept.	6	8.53	None	....	10788.2	1264.7
907 B 25	Sept.	10	7.00	None	....	385.6	55.0
907 B 26	Sept.	13	7.12	None	....	8793.1	1234.9
907 B 27	Sept.	17	13.18	None	....	381.8	28.9
907 B 28	Sept.	20	9.46	None	....	12509.6	1322.3
907 B 29	Sept.	24	7.95	None	....	209.3	26.3
907 B 30	Sept.	27	8.27	None	:...	9375.2	1133.6
907 B 31	October	1	8.30	None	....	210.7	25.3
907 B 32	October	4	6.71	None	....	7327.6	1092.0
907 B 33	October	8	7.85	None	....	162.7	20.7
907 B 34	October	11	7.40	None	....	7567.8	1022.6
907 B 35	October	15	7.50	None	....	261.7	34.8
907 B 36	October	18	6.23	None	....	5888.7	945.2

FURTHER TRIAL OF THE BORDEAUX-ARSENATE OF LEAD COMBINATION

Two trees were sprayed with Bordeaux arsenate of lead combination made after the same formula and applied in the same manner, as to tree No. 49 in 1906. The spraying was done June 21, and, in the 127 days between that date and October 26, the trees received the

Chemical Determinations from Waters Collected from Trees 1907 A and B.

Serial Number	Date	Amount of drip	Soluble constituents			
			Copper		Alkalinity in terms of calcium oxide	
			Total	Per litre	Total	Per litre
1907 A 1	June 22	1.99	29.6	14.8	78.9	39.6
1907 A 2	June 24	42.05	57.9	1.3	1104.6	26.2
1907 A 3	July 1	2.43	11.0	4.5	54.4	22.3
1907 A 4	July 6	9.50	31.4	3.3	428.1	45.0
1907 A 5	July 9, 10	25.43	88.5	3.4	267.4	10.5
1907 A 6	July 10, 11	11.04	40.0	3.6	132.4	12.0
1907 A 7	July 14, 15	23.55	90.7	3.8	178.4	7.5
1907 A 8	July 17	6.75	88.3	13.0	84.2	12.4
1907 A 9	July 26	2.54	11.5	4.5	70.9	27.9
1907 A 10	July 28	6.72	73.1	10.8	71.7	10.6
1907 A 11	July 31	17.13	121.0	7.0	131.4	7.6
1907 A 12	August 1	1.23	16.8	13.6	34.1	27.7
1907 A 13	August 5	20.60	95.0	4.6	188.6	9.1
1907 A 14	August 7	17.60	60.5	3.4	193.4	10.9
1907 A 15	August 12	5.32	34.5	6.5	42.9	8.0
1907 A 16	August 16	29.00	49.9	1.7	183.1	6.3
1907 A 17	August 17	4.89	8.9	1.8	46.8	9.4
1907 A 18	August 19	8.19	37.7	4.6	111.4	13.6
1907 A 19	Sept. 9, 10	9.42	82.1	8.7	334.4	35.4
1907 A 20	Sept. 27	7.87	79.3	10.0	Too dark	....
1907 A 21	October 3	18.38	7.8	0.4	143.9	7.8
1907 A 22	October 7	2.70	14.9	5.5	Too dark	....
1907 A 23	October 15	2.48	None	....	Too dark	....
1907 A 24	October 26	5.34	35.4	6.6	Too dark	....
1907 B 1	June 22	2.05	21.4	10.4	81.6	39.8
1907 B 2	June 24	40.90	139.8	3.4	935.3	22.8
1907 B 3	July 1	2.38	1.7	0.6	73.0	30.6
1907 B 4	July 6	9.13	61.8	6.7	171.4	18.7
1907 B 5	July 9, 10	25.44	73.4	2.8	153.1	6.0
1907 B 6	July 10, 11	10.71	19.6	1.8	94.9	8.8
1907 B 7	July 14, 15	22.56	67.6	2.9	82.4	3.6
1907 B 8	July 17	6.66	76.1	11.4	52.0	7.8
1907 B 9	July 26	2.63	1.7	0.6	20.4	7.7
1907 B 10	July 28	6.60	70.2	10.6	46.6	7.0
1907 B 11	July 31	16.08	153.6	8.3	79.5	4.9
1907 B 12	August 1	1.18	33.1	28.0	22.1	18.7
1907 B 13	August 5	19.90	62.7	3.1	182.1	9.1
1907 B 14	August 7	16.30	65.6	4.0	127.3	7.8
1907 B 15	August 12	5.17	71.2	13.7	37.6	7.2
1907 B 16	August 16	28.05	67.4	2.4	109.9	3.9
1907 B 17	August 17	4.82	15.0	3.1	43.6	9.0
1907 B 18	August 19	7.82	11.8	1.5	173.6	22.2
1907 B 19	Sept. 9, 10	7.82	82.5	10.5	Too dark	....
1907 B 20	Sept. 27	7.73	55.0	7.1	Too dark	....
1907 B 21	October 3	17.69	8.8	0.5	Too dark	....
1907 B 22	October 7	2.50	None	....	Too dark	....
1907 B 23	October 15	2.40	None	....	Too dark	....
1907 B 24	October 26	5.11	13.4	2.6	Too dark	....

waters of 24 rains. The average amount of drip collected was 11.5 litres. Of the 48 lots from the two trees, all but three contained soluble copper in measurable quantity. The maximum per litre was 28.0 milligrams; the average for the two trees 6.4 milligrams per litre. The essential differences between these trees and tree No. 49 of 1906 are that the trees of 1907 were under test for three times as long, were washed by more than twice the number of rains, and the quantities of water were nearly twice as large. The quantities of soluble copper were, however, greater in 1906 than in 1907. The maximum per litre was 3⅓ times greater in 1906. The averages were 24.2 milligrams per litre in 1906, and 6.4 milligrams per litre in 1907. The anomally in this test lies in the effect upon foliage. In 1906 there was no injury to foliage; in 1907 contrary to expectations, the leaves of both trees were conspicuously marked by brown spots and burned marginal areas. By no means all leaves were injured, many remained perfect, but the number affected was sufficient to class the injury as serious. Brown spots did not appear immediately after spraying. For a long time the leaves were without blemish. Brown spots first appeared at the same time that similar injury appeared on the leaves of the 507 trees sprayed with the Bordeaux Paris green mixture. The spots were more numerous, individual spots were larger and increase in number continued longer than was the case with the 507 trees. All circumstances, in any way connected with these tests, have been carefully canvassed, in the effort to determine the cause of injury in this particular case, but thus far it has been found impossible to isolate all the possible factors, or to secure that degree of proof necessary as a basis for definite conclusions. The injuries inflicted are identical in character with injuries produced by copper sulphate solutions, and it is believed and assumed that copper in solution was the active agent responsible for the burning. The problem is—why was serious injury inflicted when the copper in solution averaged only 6.4 milligrams per litre, while in the year previous with an average of copper in solution almost four times as large, the leaves suffered no injury? Apparently, ability to do injury does not depend upon the amount of copper in solution. That the cause of injury was not strictly local,—confined in operation to the two trees under consideration,—is shown in the concurrent appearance of injury of the same nature on the 507 and some other trees. The fact of injury, at a particular time, to all trees sprayed with Bordeaux mixture except those protected from meteoric waters, points, as in a case previously recorded, to some power inherent in falling rain, or to some particular state of the atmosphere at the time that may act directly, or indirectly, by inducing a condition of susceptibility in the trees. Results from these two trees are tabulated on page 281.

ACTION OF CARBONATED WATER

To test the action of carbon dioxide as an agent influencing the solubility of copper deposited on the leaves in Bordeaux mixture, four trees were used. These trees were equipped alike, were given the same preliminary spray of standard Bordeaux-Paris green mixture, and were provided with covers to protect from rain. One pair received the three applications of Bordeaux June 11, and between June 18 and October 15 was given 18 applications at intervals of one week, of distilled water thru which a stream of carbon dioxide had been allowed to pass for from 15 to 18 hours. The other pair received the preliminary spray of Bordeaux June 17 and, between June 25 and October 15, was sprayed 17 times, at weekly intervals with distilled water. The results from the two trees of each pair are closely approximate. Distilled water was used a little more freely than was the carbonated water and in consequence the average quantity at each application was 9.6 litres while the average for the carbonated waters was 6.6 litres. Soluble copper was present in all waters from the trees sprayed with carbonated water and in 15 of the 17 lots collected from the trees sprayed with distilled water. The average maximum of copper in solution was 25.9 milligrams per litre for the carbonated waters and 13.2 milligrams per litre for the distilled waters; the average minimum was 0.9 milligram per litre for the carbonated; 0.45 milligram per litre for the distilled waters. Considering all waters from each pair, the average was 8.2 milligrams per litre for the carbonated and 4.4 milligrams per litre for the distilled. The averages show very nearly double the amount of copper in solution in the carbonated waters, and these results, as far as they go, confirm the generally accepted opinion that carbon dioxide is an active agent in converting the copper of Bordeaux into soluble forms. The foliage of these four trees remained in perfect condition thru the season; no brown spots could be detected, and there was no yellowing of leaves. This absence of injury as in the case of other covered trees, indicates one of two things; either the amount of copper in solution is too small to be injurious, or there is some agency other than copper brought into solution thru the action of carbon dioxide, and from which these trees were defended by the covers, that is the cause, or at least, one of the causes of injury to the foliage of apple trees sprayed with Bordeaux mixture. The average amounts of copper shown to be in solution are small, but there were periods when quantities approaching the maximum found in the waters from the trees sprayed with carbonated water were present, and these amounts approximate the amounts known to be present in waters from other trees that did suffer injury.*

A further test of the influence of carbonated water may be recorded here. Two pairs of trees were sprayed alike June 17 with a Bordeaux Paris green mixture, made with a greatly reduced quantity of lime. The formula used was 4–1–¼–50. One pair of the trees was provided with covers to protect from rain, and was sprayed once each week, from June 25 to October 15, with carbonated water, in amounts that averaged 6.31 litres for each application. The number of applications was 17. The companion pair was left exposed, and, between June 22 and October 26, was subjected to 24 rains, which gave an average of 10.9 litres of water for each lot of drip collected.

*Determinations from the waters from trees 1007 A and B, sprayed with carbonated water, and from trees 1307 A and B, sprayed with distilled water, are given in tabular form on pages 284 and 285.

Copper in solution was found, in measurable quantities, in all waters from each of the four trees. The amounts in the rain waters show greater fluctuations than do those in the carbonated waters, but the averages are not widely separated. The maxima for the trees exposed to rains are 51.2 and 146.9 milligrams per litre; for the two trees sprayed with carbonated water 53.9 milligrams and 68.5 milligrams per litre. The average minimum is 1.4 milligrams per litre for the rain waters and 4.5 milligrams per litre for the carbonated waters.

Chemical Determinations from Waters Collected from Trees 1007 A and B.

Serial Number	Date	Amount of drip	Soluble constituents			
			Copper		Alkalinity in terms of calcium oxide	
			Total	Per litre	Total	Per litre
1007 A 1	June 18	7.41	5.1	0.6	160.6	21.6
1007 A 2	June 25	5.99	218.8	36.5	329.7	55.0
1007 A 3	July 2	5.38	31.4	5.8	132.9	24.7
1007 A 4	July 9	6.16	42.4	6.8	147.8	23.9
1007 A 5	July 16	6.72	54.0	8.0	435.7	64.8
1007 A 6	July 23	6.45	55.7	8.6	261.9	40.6
1007 A 7	July 30	6.80	11.0	1.6	113.9	16.7
1007 A 8	August 6	6.85	29.3	4.2	329.4	48.0
1007 A 9	August 13	5.77	31.1	5.3	87.1	15.0
1007 A 10	August 20	7.15	40.4	5.6	272.2	38.0
1007 A 11	August 27	6.66	66.9	10.0	290.5	43.6
1007 A 12	Sept. 3	6.45	54.0	8.3	181.3	28.1
1007 A 13	Sept. 10	6.40	64.8	10.1	134.0	20.9
1007 A 14	Sept. 17	6.32	60.1	9.5	104.7	16.5
1007 A 15	Sept. 24	6.55	55.0	8.3	97.1	14.8
1007 A 16	Sept. 1	6.00	61.0	10.1	Too dark	....
1007 A 17	October 8	7.00	39.3	5.6	67.0	9.5
1007 A 18	October 15	6.72	20.6	3.0	64.0	9.5
1007 B 1	June 18	8.53	9.4	1.1	184.1	21.5
1007 B 2	June 25	5.97	92.4	15.4	305.1	51.1
1007 B 3	July 2	3.05	17.5	5.7	62.0	20.3
1007 B 4	July 9	7.23	43.2	5.9	212.3	29.3
1007 B 5	July 16	9.97	110.0	11.0	105.5	10.5
1007 B 6	July 23	6.57	82.5	12.5	123.5	18.7
1007 B 7	July 30	6.83	62.5	9.1	127.1	18.6
1007 B 8	August 6	7.14	54.0	7.5	416.1	58.2
1007 B 9	August 13	6.32	32.3	5.1	66.6	10.5
1007 B 10	August 20	7.35	45.1	6.1	141.8	19.2
1007 B 11	August 27	6.90	54.0	7.8	226.0	32.7
1007 B 12	Sept. 3	6.98	54.2	7.7	234.3	33.5
1007 B 13	Sept. 10	6.55	22.0	3.3	238.1	36.3
1007 B 14	Sept. 17	6.32	100.9	15.9	131.6	20.8
1007 B 15	Sept. 24	6.55	86.4	13.1	176.1	26.8
1007 B 16	October 1	6.00	80.0	13.3	Too dark	....
1007 B 17	October 8	7.00	35.4	5.0	89.7	12.8
1007 B 18	October 15	6.82	20.2	2.0	77.4	11.3

The averages of all waters give 15.6 milligrams per litre for rain waters and 17.4 milligrams per litre for carbonated waters.

It may be concluded from this test that carbonated water has about the same solvent action upon the copper of Bordeaux as has rain water. The carbonated water acts with greater uniformity, and at no time acts with sufficient vigor to bring excessive amounts into solution. Comparing the amounts from these trees with the amounts from the trees sprayed with standard mixture and treated in like manner with carbonated water, it is apparent that reduction in lime has increased the amount of copper in solution by more than 100 percent. The amount of lime used, in the mixtures applied to these trees, is

Chemical Determinations from Waters Collected from Trees 1307 A and B.

Serial Number	Date	Amount of drip	Soluble constituents			
			Copper		Alkalinity in terms of calcium oxide	
			Total	Per litre	Total	Per litre
1307 A 1	June 25	6.96	73.5	10.5	380.6	54.6
1307 A 2	July 2	7.98	12.9	1.6	269.5	33.7
1307 A 3	July 9	9.22	9.4	1.0	312.9	33.9
1307 A 4	July 16	11.73	6.0	0.5	349.6	29.8
1307 A 5	July 23	9.98	69.5	6.9	138.6	13.8
1307 A 6	July 30	11.10	23.5	2.1	159.6	14.3
1307 A 7	August 6	11.63	83.8	7.2	158.6	13.6
1307 A 8	August 13	10.34	41.1	3.9	124.6	12.0
1307 A 9	August 20	11.10	22.0	1.9	281.6	25.3
1307 A 10	August 27	9.58	27.6	2.8	456.1	47.6
1307 A 11	Sept. 3	9.38	35.0	3.7	198.1	21.1
1307 A 12	Sept. 10	6.81	37.3	5.4	145.9	21.4
1307 A 13	Sept. 17	8.81	34.5	3.9	25.2	2.8
1307 A 14	Sept. 24	9.80	28.2	2.8	130.6	13.3
1307 A 15	October 1	9.25	22.6	2.4	145.2	15.7
1307 A 16	October 8	9.72	78.5	8.0	179.5	18.4
1307 A 17	October 15	9.22	23.2	2.5	156.7	17.0
1307 B 1	June 25	7.01	93.5	13.3	395.1	56.3
1307 B 2	July 2	8.90	4.2	0.4	193.6	21.7
1307 B 3	July 9	11.58	80.1	6.9	207.5	17.9
1307 B 4	July 16	10.33	45.3	4.3	234.4	22.6
1307 B 5	July 23	10.42	45.1	4.3	146.7	14.0
1307 B 6	July 30	11.05	None	....	89.5	8.1
1307 B 7	August 6	11.33	34.2	3.0	221.6	19.5
1307 B 8	August 13	10.50	49.5	4.7	273.7	26.0
1307 B 9	August 20	11.29	18.8	1.6	273.9	24.2
1307 B 10	August 27	10.04	47.1	4.6	328.9	32.7
1307 B 11	Sept. 3	9.90	31.4	3.1	418.7	42.2
1307 B 12	Sept. 10	9.50	46.0	4.8	227.1	23.9
1307 B 13	Sept. 17	7.20	21.6	3.0	71.4	9.9
1307 B 14	Sept. 24	8.91	60.8	6.8	117.6	13.2
1307 B 15	October 1	10.30	64.8	6.2	Too dark	....
1307 B 16	October 8	8.75	135.3	15.4	124.8	14.2
1307 B 17	October 15	7.20	None	....	97.1	13.4

very near the minimum necessary for complete precipitation of the copper. There is little if any excess. The amounts of copper in solution are greater than from any of the trees sprayed with standard Bordeaux containing equal parts by weight of copper sulphate and lime. It seems evident, therefore, that a certain excess of lime has a retarding action on the conversion of the copper of Bordeaux mixture into soluble forms.

Chemical Determinations from Waters Collected from Trees 1507 A and B.
Exposed to atmospheric conditions

Serial Number	Date	Amount of drip	Soluble constituents			
			Copper		Alkalinity in terms of calcium oxide	
			Total	Per litre	Total	Per litre
1507 A 1	June 22	1.93	67.3	34.8	74.6	38.6
1507 A 2	June 24	37.28	427.7	11.4	289.6	7.7
1507 A 3	July 1	2.19	112.7	51.4	39.4	18.0
1507 A 4	July 6	8.81	368.9	41.8	151.7	17.2
1507 A 5	July 9, 10	23.73	384.5	16.2	37.2	1.5
1507 A 6	July 10, 11	9.99	125.2	12.6	72.7	7.2
1507 A 7	July 14, 15	21.51	24.0	1.1	140.5	6.5
1507 A 8	July 17	6.68	78.6	11.7	102.6	15.3
1507 A 9	July 26	2.28	47.0	20.6	Too dark	....
1507 A 10	July 28	5.70	66.0	11.5	17.7	3.1
1507 A 11	July 31	15.07	127.2	8.4	28.3	1.8
1507 A 12	August 1	1.04	28.7	22.7	7.1	6.8
1507 A 13	August 5	18.72	62.4	3.3	97.8	5.2
1507 A 14	August 7	16.45	79.8	4.8	98.9	6.0
1507 A 15	August 11	4.65	44.4	9.5	19.7	4.2
1507 A 16	August 16	22.65	52.3	2.3	76.1	3.3
1507 A 17	August 17	4.39	39.3	8.9	40.2	9.1
1507 A 18	August 19	7.68	34.7	4.5	121.5	15.8
1507 A 19	Sept. 9, 10	8.03	65.8	8.1	Too dark	....
1507 A 20	Sept. 27	7.04	76.6	10.8	Too dark	....
1507 A 21	October 3	16.42	212.0	12.8	Too dark	....
1507 A 22	October 7	2.30	18.8	8.1	Too dark	....
1507 A 23	October 15	2.30	39.3	17.0	Too dark	....
1507 A 24	October 26	4.98	13.7	2.7	Too dark	....
1507 B 1	June 22	1.83	177.6	97.0	84.1	45.9
1507 B 2	June 24	37.25	444.0	11.9	317.1	8.5
1507 B 3	July 1	2.30	337.3	146.6	24.7	10.7
1507 B 4	July 6	9.32	452.1	48.5	68.0	7.2
1507 B 5	July 9, 10	24.70	127.6	5.1	475.3	19.2
1507 B 6	July 10, 11	10.39	105.0	10.1	161.2	15.5
1507 B 7	July 14, 15	22.89	174.8	7.6	527.3	23.0
1507 B 8	July 17	7.13	43.2	6.0	304.3	42.6
1507 B 9	July 26	2.44	5.6	2.2	13.6	5.5
1507 B 10	July 28	6.47	24.9	3.8	74.0	11.4
1507 B 11	July 31	16.56	78.9	4.7	172.6	10.4
1507 B 12	August 1	1.11	16.1	14.5	60.6	54.6
1507 B 13	August 5	19.35	55.0	2.8	126.4	6.5
1507 B 14	August 7	17.15.	31.4	1.8	84.2	4.9
1507 B 15	August 11	5.10	55.5	10.8	70.6	13.8
1507 B 16	August 16	28.50	76.8	2.6	66.9	2.3
1507 B 17	August 17	4.73	15.5	3.2	24.5	5.1
1507 B 18	August 19	7.50	16.5	2.2	196.2	26.1
1507 B 19	Sept. 9, 10	8.62	43.2	5.0	Too dark	....
1507 B 20	Sept. 27	7.45	36.6	4.9	Too dark	....
1507 B 21	October 3	17.34	106.1	6.1	Too dark	....
1507 B 22	October 7	2.50	7.9	3.1	Too dark	....
1507 B 23	October 15	2.32	7.8	3.3	Too dark	....
1507 B 24	October 26	4.69	14.7	3.1	Too dark	....

Turning now to the effects on foliage of this reduction in lime, it may be stated that the foliage of the trees exposed to rains was very seriously injured. Brown spots appeared immediately following the first rain. The injury continued to increase, and a large part of the leaves dropped off. Of leaves remaining at the close of the season, practically all were in a damaged condition.

•Chemical Determinations from Waters Collected from Trees 1707 A and B.
Protected from rain; sprayed with carbonated water

Serial Number	Date		Amount of drip	Soluble constituents			
				Copper		Alkalinity in terms of calcium oxide	
				Total	Per litre	Total	Per litre
1707 A 1	June	25	8.97	228.0	25.4	344.6	38.4
1707 A 2	July	2	5.51	297.0	53.9	38.5	6.9
1707 A 3	July	9	6.44	59.7	9.2	85.3	13.2
1707 A 4	July	16	5.67	233.3	41.1	85.8	15.1
1707 A 5	July	23	6.82	190.1	27.8	83.2	12.2
1707 A 6	July	30	6.13	123.7	20.1	74.8	12.2
1707 A 7	August	6	6.60	92.3	14.0	75.9	11.5
1707 A 8	August	13	6.19	34.5	5.5	30.3	4.8
1707 A 9	August	20	6.32	86.3	13.8	189.5	30.0
1707 A 10	August	27	6.19	131.2	21.1	115.6	18.6
1707 A 11	Sept.	3	7.06	85.3	12.0	147.6	20.9
1707 A 12	Sept.	10	6.21	103.6	16.6	145.0	23.3
1707 A 13	Sept.	17	6.26	110.0	17.5	Too dark	....
1707 A 14	Sept.	24	6.38	71.9	11.2	86.7	13.5
1707 A 15	October	1	6.10	69.1	11.3	50.9	8.3
1707 A 16	October	8	6.30	42.4	6.7	Too dark	....
1707 A 17	October	15	6.13	50.0	8.1	32.1	5.2
1707 B 1	June	25	4.98	71.5	14.3	58.6	11.7
1707 B 2	July	2	4.95	339.5	68.5	22.5	4.5
1707 B 3	July	9	8.25	113.8	13.7	112.2	13.6
1707 B 4	July	16	5.67	171.7	30.4	126.9	22.3
1707 B 5	July	23	5.61	137.5	24.5	84.7	15.0
1707 B 6	July	30	6.18	102.4	16.5	65.9	10.6
1707 B 7	August	6	6.40	67.4	10.5	79.5	12.4
1707 B 8	August	13	6.56	67.5	10.2	64.3	9.8
1707 B 9	August	20	7.20	101.9	14.1	210.9	29.2
1707 B 10	August	27	6.47	77.8	12.0	89.9	13.8
1707 B 11	Sept.	3	5.86	69.1	11.7	103.3	17.6
1707 B 12	Sept.	10	5.28	34.9	6.6	Too dark	....
1707 B 13	Sept.	17	5.96	62.8	10.5	Too dark	....
1707 B 14	Sept.	24	6.38	66.5	10.4	Too dark	....
1707 B 15	October	1	6.50	67.1	10.3	Too dark	....
1707 B 16	October	8	7.07	25.2	3.5	76.1	10.7
1707 B 17	October	15	6.02	47.1	7.8	35.5	5.8

The foliage, on the trees sprayed with carbonated water, remained perfect for a considerable time, but early in September a few of the lower leaves became slightly spotted. This injury did not increase, and the general condition of foliage at the close of the season was rated as excellent. In the matter of adhesiveness, the four trees were alike. They served as an excellent illustration of the relation of proper excess of lime to adhesiveness. When sprayed, the trees were of the normal

Bordeaux blue color. But, at each washing with rain or carbonated water, this color was diminished and by the first of September only slight traces of the mixture was diminished and by the first of September only slight traces of the mixture could be found on the leaves. On all the trees, leaves assumed the dark green shades that have been referred to in connection with some other trees, but the blue color retained thruout the season by leaves of trees sprayed with Bordeaux having the full complement of lime was entirely wanting or only present in a few small spots.

Tabulations of the chemical data obtained from the waters from the trees used in this test of carbonated waters are given on pages 286 and 287.

BORDEAUX MADE WITH AIR-SLAKED LIME

The danger in using air-slaked lime has been referred to; but brief mention may here be made of the results obtained from two trees treated with a Bordeaux-Paris green mixture, made after the standard formula, but in which air-slaked, instead of fresh-slaked lime was used. The three applications were made June 19. Drip Waters, from the 24 rains that fell between June 19 and October 26, were collected, and examined for copper in solution. The mixture at time of application contained no soluble copper. Measurable quantities of copper in solution were found in all waters collected, but the amounts were less than was anticipated. The maximum was 70 milligrams per litre, the same as was found for the waters from the No. 507 trees. The average copper in solution was 8.9 milligrams per litre for the two trees here considered, while for the No. 507 trees it was 9.2 milligrams per litre. This is a fairly close approximation for these two pairs of trees in this matter of copper in solution. The striking differences between the two pairs of trees were:

1. In amount of injury to foliage. The injury appearing on leaves of the No. 507 trees has been described as slight, and as first appearing 62 days after application of the spray. The injury to foliage of the two trees treated with Bordeaux made with air-slaked lime was very serious, resulting in the early loss of a large portion of the leaves. Brown spots appeared in considerable numbers immediately following the first rain June 22, and the injury continued to increase for several weeks. Many leaves became wholly brown and promptly dropped off. It is recorded in the notes made September 4—that fully half the leaves had then fallen and those remaining were, almost without exception, more or less injured by brown spots.

2. In regard to adhesiveness. Bordeaux applied to the No. 507 trees was as adhesive as possible; spots or splashes having the normal Bordeaux blue color remained on practically all leaves, and many were still completely coated at the close of the season.

On the other pair the air-slaked lime Bordeaux did not give to the leaves a normal color when applied. It lacked the bright blue characteristic of well made mixtures and appeared dull and dingy. Each rain reduced the color perceptibly and by the first of August there remained only a few small spots on some of the leaves. In fact casual examin-

Chemical Determinations from Waters Collected from Trees 1407 A and B.

Serial Number	Date	Amount of drip	Soluble constituents			
			Copper		Alkalinity in terms of calcium oxide	
			Total	Per litre	Total	Per litre
1407 A 1	June 22	2.01	140.4	69.8	78.3	38.9
1407 A 2	June 24	39.15	194.2	4.9	467.7	11.9
1407 A 3	July 1	2.47	34.4	13.9	45.7	18.5
1407 A 4	July 6	8.49	58.8	6.9	193.5	22.7
1407 A 5	July 9	25.34	189.2	7.4	145.7	5.7
1407 A 6	July 10, 11	10.07	110.0	10.8	123.7	12.2
1407 A 7	July 14, 15	23.39	90.0	3.8	410.0	17.5
1407 A 8	July 17	6.83	68.3	10.0	72.7	10.6
1407 A 9	July 26	2.61	11.7	4.4	31.7	12.1
1407 A 10	July 28	6.85	110.5	16.1	19.6	2.8
1407 A 11	July 31	17.13	106.1	6.1	80.1	4.6
1407 A 12	August 1	1.10	43.2	39.2	7.4	6.7
1407 A 13	August 5	20.63	152.7	7.4	112.5	5.4
1407 A 14	August 7	17.29	116.6	6.7	81.1	4.6
1407 A 15	August 11	5.16	56.1	10.8	39.7	7.6
1407 A 16	August 16	29.07	89.4	3.0	175.8	6.0
1407 A 17	August 17	4.81	18.9	3.9	41.3	8.5
1407 A 18	August 19	8.13	60.0	7.3	103.1	12.6
1407 A 19	Sept. 9, 10	8.26	47.1	5.7	Too dark	....
1407 A 20	Sept. 27	7.64	Lost	Lost	Too dark	....
1407 A 21	October 3	17.78	49.1	2.8	Too dark	....
1407 A 22	October 7	2.55	15.7	6.1	Too dark	....
1407 A 23	October 15	2.50	11.0	4.4	Too dark	....
1407 A 24	October 26	4.93	39.4	7.9	Too dark	....
1407 B 1	June 22	2.17	54.2	24.9	98.7	45.4
1407 B 2	June 24	41.04	127.3	3.1	461.7	11.2
1407 B 3	July 1	2.27	3.9	1.7	32.9	14.4
1407 B 4	July 6	9.01	46.8	5.0	223.5	24.8
1407 B 5	July 9	25.64	154.0	6.0	147.5	5.7
1407 B 6	July 10, 11	10.81	77.7	7.1	294.9	27.2
1407 B 7	July 14, 15	23.04	31.4	1.3	150.5	6.5
1407 B 8	July 17	6.92	47.4	6.8	82.9	11.9
1407 B 9	July 26	2.86	26.7	9.3	70.6	24.6
1407 B 10	July 28	6.94	59.0	8.5	14.5	2.0
1407 B 11	July 31	17.28	106.1	6.1	49.4	2.8
1407 B 12	August 1	1.19	28.7	24.1	15.7	13.1
1407 B 13	August 5	20.60	72.3	3.5	137.4	6.6
1407 B 14	August 7	17.33	60.0	3.4	141.2	8.1
1407 B 15	August 11	5.32	57.0	10.7	113.5	21.3
1407 B 16	August 16	29.20	51.6	1.7	259.6	8.8
1407 B 17	August 17	5.00	3.4	0.6	78.5	15.7
1407 B 18	August 19	7.95	16.0	2.0	49.7	6.2
1407 B 19	Sept. 9, 10	9.62	49.5	5.1	Too dark	....
1407 B 20	Sept. 27	7.81	47.1	6.0	Too dark	....
1407 B 21	October 3	17.88	18.8	1.0	Too dark	....
1407 B 22	October 7	2.75	15.5	5.6	Too dark	....
1407 B 23	October 15	2.55	9.4	3.6	7.8	3.0
1407 B 24	October 26	5.28	13.4	2.5	Too dark	....

ation at this time gave the impression that the trees had not been sprayed.

Soluble copper, however, continued to appear in the waters collected, and in amounts averaging about 20 percent above the average for all waters. It appears that all surplus lime and all calcium sulphate were quickly washed away, leaving a considerable amount of copper upon the trees. That this copper was in some slowly soluble form is shown by the small amounts given up to the waters passing over the trees; that it possessed considerable adhesiveness is apparent from its regular appearance during more than 2½ months from the time of practical disappearance of the blue color; that it possessed the power to act injuriously upon leaves, the continued loss of foliage thru burning fully testified. The chemical data necessary to the satisfactory solution of several questions that are suggested by the behavior of the mixture applied to these trees are not at hand, and these questions must be added to the already long list of matters demanding further investigation.

It is a further fact regarding these trees, that uninjured portions of leaves assumed a very dark green color, as was determined by comparison with leaves from other sprayed trees and from trees that had not been sprayed. Determinations of copper in solution in waters collected from the trees sprayed with air-slaked lime, are given in tabular form page 289.

SOLUBILITY OF COPPER UNDER THE INFLUENCE OF LONG CONTINUED
MOIST CONDITIONS AND UNDER SPRAY APPLIED AT FREQUENT
INTERVALS

Certain irregularities in the amounts of copper found in solution in the waters, collected from trees in 1906, brought up the question— Does the copper become soluble gradually and accumulate as soluble copper on the leaves during intervals between rains or sprays, or is it made soluble under the direct action of the water passing over the leaves?

To obtain information on this matter, two trees were prepared with covers to protect from rain, and with the arrangements for collecting waters sprayed over the leaves. Both trees were given three heavy applications of standard Bordeaux-Paris green mixture on June 17. It was proposed that after an interval of a few days, one tree should be sprayed, allowed to dry, then sprayed again and this repeated as many times as possible during the day. The other tree to be kept continuously wet during a day, with a final spray at night. These treatments were to be repeated at intervals thru the season. Because of the large amount of work demanded by the numerous experiments in progress it was found impossible to carry out the original plan. Only two all-day treatments were given, the first July 22, thirty-five days after the trees had received the coating of Bordeaux, and the second August 28, after an interval of 37 days. At 8:00 a. m. July 22, one tree was sprayed with about seven litres of cistern water, the jar emptied and the tree allowed to dry. It was found that one hour

served to fully dry the foliage. A second application was made at
9:00 a. m. and others followed at one hour intervals. Ten lots of
water were taken during the day. Commencing at the same time in
the morning the other tree was sprayed with just enough water to
moisten the leaves, and additional applications were made with such
frequency that a continually wet condition of the leaves was maintained
thruout the day. As little water as possible was used, but small quantities continually dripped into the jar and at evening the amount collected amounted to nearly nine litres. This water was removed and
then the tree was sprayed with about 7 litres, which was also con-

Chemical Determinations from Waters Collected from Trees 1107 A and 1107 B.

Serial Number	Date		Amount of drip	Soluble constituents			
				Copper		Alkalinity in terms of calcium oxide	
				Total	Per litre	Total	Per litre
1107 A 1	July	22	6.93	6.2	0.8 .	194.9	28.1
1107 A · 2	July	22	7.39	15.3	2.0	. 127.7	17.2
1107 A 3	July	22	6.68	23.9	3.5	113.0	16.9
1107 A 4	July ·	22	6.95	10.5	1.5	110.7	15.9
1107 A 5	July	22	6.69	18.6	2.7	96.1	14.3
1107 A 6	July	22	6.85	1.7	0.2	78.8	11.5
1107 A 7	July	22	6.55	5.3	0.8	80.3	12.2
1107 A 8	July	22	7.66	18.8	2.4	84.0	10.9
1107 A 9	July	22	5.90	None	....	103.4	17.5
1107 A 10	July	22	7.82	None	....	150.9	19.2
1107 A 11	August	28	7.56	64.8	8.5	230.5	30.4
1107 A 12	August	28	7.85	14.1	1.8	208.8	26.5
1107 A 13	August	28	6.96	14.7	2.1	109.1	15.6
1107 A 14	August	28	8.56	31.1	3.6	145.2	16.9
1107 A 15	August	28	9.39	21.7	2.3	161.4	17.1
1107 A 16	August	28	11.00	None	....	149.6	13.6
1107 A 17	August	28	6.45	13.8	2.1	106.2	16.4
1107 A 18	August	28	9.70	11.3	1.1	272.1	28.0
1107 A 19	August	28	8.37	18.8	2.2	141.8	16.9
1107 B 1	July	22	8.81	23.1	2.6	204.8	23.2
1107 B 2	July	22	6.96	Lost	....	211.7	30.5
1107 B 3	August	28	12.70	70.7	5.5	385.8	30.3
1107 B 4	August	28	8.75	None	....	145.0	16.5

lected and reserved for analysis. August 28, the same procedure was
repeated, except that only 9 waters were collected from the tree
sprayed at 1 hour intervals.

The average of all lots of water, collected from the trees, sprayed
at one hour intervals, was 7.68 litres. Copper was found in solution
in lots 1 to 8 July 22. Lots 9 and 10 contained none. Of the waters
August 28—all except the sixth contained copper in solution. The
amounts were small in all waters. The maximum of July 22 was 3.5
milligrams per litre in the third lot. August 28 the maximum 8.5
milligrams per litre appeared in the first water. Succeeding amounts
ranged between 1.1 milligrams per litre in the eighth and 3.6 milligrams

per litre in the fourth. Lot No. 9 the last, contained 2.2 milligrams per litre. The average was 1.77 milligrams per litre on the earlier date and 2.97 milligrams on August 28.

The small amount of copper in solution (0.8 milligrams per litre) in the first water of July 22, indicates that no process of conversion of copper to soluble forms could have been in operation during the 35 days from application of the Bordeaux to first spraying with water. That some conversion took place in the interval between July 22 and August 28 is indicated by the fact that more than one third of the total copper found in the nine waters was recovered from the first lot of water collected. Subsequent waters, except the sixth, contained small amounts but enough to show that the solvent action takes place under direct applications. The uniformly small amounts of copper, appearing in solution, attest the slow solubility of the Bordeaux, under the conditions imposed in this test.

The water from the tree, kept continually moist July 22, yielded 2.6 milligrams of soluble copper per litre. The water from the after spray was lost through accident. On the later date, the drip accumulated during the day gave 5.5 milligrams per litre, and the lot of water from the after spray contained no copper. Apparently a long continued moist condition of foliage maintained by water applied as a spray does not increase the solubility of the copper in Bordeaux to any appreciable extent. The foliage of the two trees remained in perfect condition during the test. Determinations of soluble copper and lime are given in tabular form page 291.

CONCLUSIONS

The observations and experiments recorded in the foregoing pages are presented as a report of progress of an investigation of Bordeaux mixture in its relations to orchard trees and particularly with reference to its effects upon foliage.

The primary problem is complex, presenting several distinct phases. Each of these phases when subjected to definite experiments broadened and subdivided until the field of the investigation extended beyond anticipated limits. Some of the lines of experiments have given results from which fairly definite conclusions were possible. Other lines of experiments have been characterized by anomalous or directly contradictory results that have proved perplexing, difficult to interpret and that demanded repetition or extension of the experiments instead of leading to definite conclusions. Such results have occurred rather frequently and are ascribed, in great part, to the intimate relations between variable and interdependent factors that are difficult to isolate; such as the phenomena included under the term atmospheric conditions.

Where conflict and obscurity attend the results of experiments, it is only by repetition and continued observation of accompanying circumstances that reasons for conflicts can be determined and the uncertainties that stand in the way of definite conclusions cleared away.

This procedure requires time and sufficiently explains why the investigation has been prolonged and why it must be continued in order to reach satisfactory conclusions on the many points involved.

Owing to the exacting nature of the details attending the somewhat extended experiments relating to soluble copper in waters from sprayed trees, other phases of the problem have been held in abeyance or have received but little attention. Investigation of these phases will be pushed during the present season and it is hoped that definite conclusions may be reached regarding some of the important questions involved.

The subjects discussed in the present paper may be epitomized as follows:

1. Injury to foliage of apple trees following applications of Bordeaux mixture is of common occurrence. Much of the injury reported or observed is preventable. The principal sources of injury as determined by observation are—

    1. Use of impure or improper materials.
    2. Carelessness in making the mixtures.
    3. Improper and ineffective application.

The first two of these sources of difficulty can be entirely eliminated and the third greatly mitigated by reasonable attention and supervision. Formulas must be respected and small details of practice must receive attention in order to attain best results.

But when all precautions have been taken injury sometimes results. These non-preventable injuries are associated with unfortunate weather conditions and particularly with the action of rain and dew.

2. The chemical changes occurring in making Bordeaux mixture are still involved in some obscurity. That the copper is deposited in the form of copper hydroxide, as has been generally accepted, is denied by Professor Pickering who also points out the difficulty attending analysis of the precipitate formed.

3. The adhesiveness of Bordeaux mixture depends very much upon the manner of making and upon the character of the lime used. Variation in the proportions of copper sulphate and lime beyond certain well-defined limits decreases adhesiveness. With lime of good quality a close approximation of equal parts. of copper sulphate and lime gives greatest adhesiveness.

There is decided advantage in the maintenance of an excess of lime upon the foliage, but this must be accomplished by subsequent applications and not by increasing the amount in the original mixture.

4. No definite experiments regarding the accumulation of copper in the soil under sprayed trees have been conducted, but from results reported of experiments of others it does not appear that there is danger from this source. There is no evidence at hand that in any way associates browning or yellowing of foliage with copper in the soil.

5. The two classes of leaf injury considered are, "Brown-spotting" and "Yellowing." Brown-spotting is the more common injury.

Yellowing, when it appears in epidemic form, is the more serious of the two because affected leaves are entirely destroyed.

Not all brown-spotting is due to spraying. Other causes are, frosts, winds accompanying cold spring storms, fungi and insects.

Leaf injuries are most common and most serious in neglected orchards. Much of the injury following spraying is attributable to abrasions of the epidermis made by insects, and to infection by fungi preceding spraying.

6. The ideal spray compound that is perfectly effective and at the same time perfectly harmless on all occasions and under all conditions has not yet been discovered. Bordeaux mixture most nearly approximates the ideal, but its harmlessness can not be absolutely depended upon.

7. Injuries to foliage do sometimes follow applications of Bordeaux mixture and appear to be unavoidable. There are differences of opinion as to the exact manner in which injuries are inflicted. The important questions involved are: 1—The agencies thru which copper deposited on the leaves become soluble, and 2—The manner in which the toxic action is communicated to the cell protoplasm. The carbon dioxide contained in the air and in meteoric waters is accepted as an active agent in rendering soluble the copper of Bordeaux mixture and it is believed that the ammonium compounds brought down by rain may also exert a solvent action on the copper.

8. Laboratory experiments gave results showing that the copper of Bordeaux mixture remained insoluble for long periods. These results accord with the results of similar laboratory experiments reported by Millardet and Gayon and on which they based their claim that the copper of Bordeaux mixture, as deposited on leaves, remains insoluble as long as free lime is present.

Field experiments, however, directly contradict the laboratory results and show conclusively that, under orchard conditions, copper, in small quantity, becomes soluble very soon after deposition and continues to appear as long as any of the mixture remains upon the leaves. The presence of lime in excess does not prevent solution of the copper.

9. No evidence has been obtained in support of the suggestions of authors that solution of copper occurs thru the agency of germinating spores, or thru secretions from leaf surfaces.

10. Actual demonstration of the presence of copper in dead leaf cells has not been made, but the theory of penetration and of death of cell protoplasm by direct contact with copper is regarded as more probable than the theory of transmission of toxic effect without penetration as advanced by Rumm.

11. The value of Bordeaux mixture as a fungicide depends upon the contained copper. The action is preventive and not curative. It follows that early application with the one aim of defense gives infinitely better results than later application intended to check ravages already begun.

12. Spores of different fungi resist the action of copper in varying degrees. Millardet and Gayon found that solutions of copper

sulphate 2 or 3:10,000,000 would prevent infection by zoospores of grape mildew. Our tests with spores of the apple scab fungus show that solutions of copper sulphate 1:100,000 slightly retard germination and that the concentration necessary to entirely prevent germination lies between 1:25,000 and 1:10,000.

In the stronger solution some of the common moulds grew with apparently undiminished vigor.

13. The causes of yellowing of leaves of apple trees are obscure and not well understood. From observations extending over five seasons it seems certain that there are several causes which may operate singly, or together. Recurrent epidemics of yellowing appear to have no direct relation to wet or dry periods, or to other weather conditions. The experiments made do not establish any direct and positive connection between spraying with well-made Bordeaux mixture and yellowing of leaves, but do show that improperly made mixtures may cause yellowing and that yellowing results from use of simple solutions of copper sulphate.

14. Healthy bark of apple trees is impermeable to Bordeaux mixture and solutions of copper sulphate. Copper sulphate solutions are absorbed thru wounds and promptly kill the leaves which then become brown. Numerous experiments in which copper sulphate solutions varying from 1:100 to 1:1,000 were injected thru roots and thru holes bored in trunks of trees, uniformly resulted in browning of leaves. The copper penetrates to the leaves as was determined by analysis. The time required to give evidence of injury varies with the strength of the solution and the rate of transpiration, but is usually short, varying from 25 minutes in one case to several hours where the weaker solutions were used. A further series of experiments in which much less concentrated solutions were used was commenced rather late in the season and is to be repeated this year. One tree in this series supplied with a solution of copper sulphate 1:25,000 developed unmistakable yellowing of leaves on branches situated in the direct track of the ascending solution.

15. The importance of rain and dew as agents causing brown-spotting of foliage following applications of Bordeaux mixture is well attested by the uniform results obtained from the experiments with covered and uncovered trees. Two trees were sprayed heavily; one was left exposed, the other was protected from all rain and dew. This was repeated during three seasons. In each year the foliage of the exposed tree was more or less injured by brown spots, while the tree protected from rain remained free from injury.

Several other experiments in which trees exposed to rain were brought into contrast with trees protected from rain gave, in all cases, the same results, namely, some degree of injury to foliage exposed to rain and absolute freedom from injury to the foliage of trees protected from rain.

16. Milk of lime does not cause brown spots even when applied in large quantity, but burning quickly follows applications of copper

sulphate solutions even when the solutions are very dilute. It is therefore concluded that copper in solution is the active agent responsible for the burning of foliage.

17. From comparisons between leaves sprayed with Bordeaux mixture and milk of lime, with Bordeaux mixture only, with milk of lime only, and leaves that had not been sprayed it was found that all leaves on which lime had been used were distinctly larger than those receiving no milk of lime. This suggests a stimulating action on the part of the lime, whether by direct action on the leaves, or by reason of the protective covering afforded has not been determined.

18. Bordeaux mixture has a decided influence upon the color of leaves. Under a coating of Bordeaux mixture leaves assume a very dark green color that is retained even after the coating is mostly washed away. Leaves coated with lime only become in some degree darker in color than untreated leaves, but the shade is not so deep as is assumed under a coating of Bordeaux mixture.

19. The frequently expressed opinions that character of the storm influences the rate of solution and the amount of soluble copper on leaves, and the suggestion that electrical storms tend to increase the amount of copper in solution and the subsequent injury to foliage gain no support from the results of our experiments. There appears to be no correlation between the character of the storm and the rate of solubility or the amount of copper found in solution in the waters collected from sprayed trees. Neither is there any evidence that electrical storms increase the amounts of copper in solution.

ACKNOWLEDGMENTS

From the beginning of this investigation of Bordeaux mixture it was understood that the problems to be solved were largely chemical rather than horticultural and that the cooperation of a chemist would be necessary. In July 1906 the services of Mr. O. S. Watkins were secured and he began work, under the direction of Dr. H. S. Grindley, in one of the laboratories of the department of chemistry of the University. As the work progressed and extensions were decided upon, a laboratory within the department of horticulture and especially equipped for the work was deemed essential to rapid and satisfactory conduct of the investigation. In the spring of 1907 such a laboratory was provided. Since the installation of necessary apparatus all determinations of copper have been made by an electrolytic process.

All determinations tabulated in connection with experiments given in detail in preceding pages were made by Mr. Watkins who has been in charge of the laboratory and who has also rendered efficient aid in the conduct of field work. The writer is also under many obligations to Dr. H. S. Grindley for frequent counsel and advice in matters touching the chemical phases of the problems undertaken.